Cowboys, Miners, Presidents & Kings

The Story of the
Grand Canyon
Railway

by Al Richmond

FOURTH EDITION

Fourth Edition

Cowboys, Miners, Presidents and Kings; the Story of The Grand
Canyon Railway   ISBN 0-933269-02-1 Softcover
                      ISBN 0-933269-03-X Hardcover

Cover Photo: A 3500 class locomotive with trailing varnish makes its way through a northern Arizona snow.
George A. Duffield Collection

PUBLISHED BY:
GRAND CANYON RAILWAY

Cover Design By:
Sullivan Santamaria Design

Illustrations By:
Gini Alexander

Photography and Photo Copying By:
Al Richmond

Photographic Printing By:
Charles W. Suran Jr.

Production By:
Northland Graphics

DEDICATION

This history would not have been possible to write without the help and support of many people. It is to these people who willingly gave of their time and knowledge and especially to those people who lived this history and are no longer with us that this record is offered.

CONTENTS

PREFACE

This is not an inventory of sixty-five miles of track, ties and track spikes. It is a recognition of the people, events, circumstances, culture and equipment all of which made up the daily operation of the Grand Canyon Railway. The line became a part of a larger railroad and instead of being swallowed by the system, supported it with the notoriety provided by its destination.

Cowboys, miners, presidents and kings all played a part with this railroad. Yet these are only a few of the many people from vastly different backgrounds who built, worked for, worked around, worked with, depended on and rode this line or transported people and goods from Williams to the Grand Canyon. It appeared to have a life of its own from the start. The Canyon line lived in the hearts of the people around it. When it shut down as a result of dwindling revenues, it never really died for the railroad continued to live in the memories of those who had been close to it.

As it is with people who lie in the sun, the railway merely slept. And now, its sleep is over. The Grand Canyon Railway is awake again and writing new history. New friends and memories are being made again. This is the way it should be.

Stop off
and visit the

Grand Canyon
National Park

Santa Fe

GETTING UP STEAM

Millions of years before humans walked the Earth, geologic and climatological forces combined to shape one of the Seven Wonders of the world, the Grand Canyon. A major upheaval produced by tectonic forces, rapid downcutting by a primal river system, volcanic episodes and generations of biological changes all became a part of the attraction which draws millions of people to its rim every year.

Because of its immensity and precipitous flanks the Canyon became either a home or a barrier to the first human inhabitants. Spanish conquistadors "discovered" it in the 16th century and recorded its presence and their feelings of awe for posterity. From that time until the late 1800s the Grand Canyon remained unexplored and a blank spot on the maps of North America. It lay far removed from population centers and major routes of travel. John Wesley Powell's two voyages of exploration on the Colorado River through the Canyon changed all of that. His reports and newspaper articles of his travels brought attention to the Colorado Plateau, the Grand Canyon and in effect, opened the region to further exploration and settlement.

During the sequences of deposition and erosion vast stores of mineral wealth became incorporated in this most marvelous of landscapes and in turn climate exposed them. Sequences of freezing, thawing and erosion by wind and water allowed prospectors a brief glimpse into the riches waiting for those smart and strong enough to get at them. The Canyon and the region to the south hold rewards for the industrious and tricks for the unwary.

By the 1880s people began to realize the potential of this diverse landscape and tap its resources. Ranchers and

1

William Owen "Buckey" O'Neill, Captain in the Rough Riders. This photograph was taken in New York just prior to his departure for Cuba. Lombard Collection, NAU

prospectors moved into the region. Cattle and sheep thrived on the grasses. The Francis Mining District to the south became a classic scene of men searching for instant riches. Hard working men knew fortunes existed in and on the earth and many did their best to retrieve them. In later years others would mine the pockets of tourists who flock to the rim in greater numbers with each passing year.

How to unlock the mineral wealth of the Francis Mining District? How to get cattle and sheep to market? How to get people to the Grand Canyon? How? How? In the late eighteen hundreds these questions plagued miners, travelers, prospectors, ranchers, promoters, legislators of the Arizona Territorial Legislature and newspaper editors alike. All had the same ideas and dreams. Only one answer made any sense. A railroad!

Problem was in the early 1880s railroads did not exist in northern Arizona. Until then travel had been by horse, mule, foot, wagon or stage. Camels made their way across the scene back in the 1850s when Lieutenant Edward F. Beale made his survey through the area. Travelers to the Grand Canyon in these early years had no fast and easy means of transportation available.

Anyone shipping cattle or sheep drove them many miles to railheads or grazing areas. Not too profitable. A prospector who found what he believed to be instant wealth soon realized he could not ship his ore except by wagon. No profit there either. Very few willing tourists in those early days traveled to the Grand

Canyon and those who did found horses and wagons the only means available for the several day round trip from Flagstaff, Williams or Ash Fork. These accommodations brought small returns for the livery and stage operators and proved very tiresome for the travelers.

When the Atlantic and Pacific Railroad made its way into the area in the summer of 1882, it represented a great improvement in transportation for the residents of the region. However, this east-west enterprise had no intentions of going to the Grand Canyon.

Certainly the A&P made it a tad easier for the ranchers who now only had to drive their cattle and sheep to the nearest loading point on the main line. Every little bit of distance cut off saved time, money and helped to ensure the cattle arrived at market in better condition. Miner's ore wagons made a better time of it also. Their haul to the main line now being considerably reduced they finally made a small profit. Tourists remained the only ones left to the old ways.

Everyone sensed money was out there to be made. Promoters could smell it. When legal or illegal mining ventures could make a buck pressure was usually brought to bear on the governor and the legislature. "The Territory of Arizona needs more railroads!" became the cry of the day. "We've got to have them yesterday! Why are you lawmakers just sitting on your duffs and

J. DuPratt White (l.), and Buckey O'Neill (r.), watch Thomas R. Lombard cook dinner in a silver chafing dish at the Grand Canyon.

Lombard Collection, NAU

3

City of Williams about 1901 with Santa Fe Pacific railroad yards in the foreground.   Williams City Library Collection

not doing anything about it? There's money in the ground and the only way to get it out is by railroad!"

Jumping on the bandwagon, as if it had any choice, the 15th Territorial Legislature enacted tax exemptions in 1887 giving any company building a railroad in Arizona freedom from property taxation for six years. The lawmakers even specifically mentioned a railroad from the Atlantic and Pacific line to the Grand Canyon. This action interested a few people and railroads were built, but not in northern Arizona. Tourism to the Grand Canyon did not seem like something profitable and besides, plenty of other mines operated in central and southern Arizona. The livery, stage and freight companies could handle the exisiting traffic. Why bother to spend the money?

Why bother indeed? When prospectors from the Francis Mining District south of the Grand Canyon started showing up at assay offices with copper ore richer than any ever seen in Arizona, people began to change their minds. Montana Senator Williams Andrew Clark of the United Verde Copper Company which had vastly rich holdings in Jerome, Arizona Territory became a proponent and his engineers began to stake claims in the Francis district.

In the early 1890s copper was king in Arizona. Enthusiastic stories of the gold and silver mines appeared in the press and men talked of them over drinks or card games in the bars and saloons but copper remained the big money maker. Copper ore is far more abundant and it is easier and less expensive to mine than

4

gold or silver. But no one jumped at the chance and built the railroad to the Canyon. Even with someone like Clark expressing interest a general reluctance to part with investment capital for the railroad prevailed. His company did work the Copper Queen mines in the Anita area after the railroad came into being.

About 1893, William O. "Buckey" O'Neill, son of Ireland, mayor of Prescott, legendary sheriff of Yavapai County, prospector, promoter and later to become one of Teddy Roosevelt's Rough Riders, realized money could be made in the mining and railroad business between Williams and the Grand Canyon. He had a number of good claims and backed some others in what would become the Anita area. O'Neill actually had several of his claims in the Grand Canyon proper and built a substantial cabin on the south rim. To get at this wealth he needed money for development. However, there wasn't enough in the vicinity to buy a good bottle of whiskey. At least so it seemed.

Buckey began to check around. Virtually all of the big, available money was back east. That being the case he packed up his ore samples and headed for the eastern financial districts. He knocked on a lot of doors with little or no success until he came across the investment firm of Lombard, Goode and Company in New York. This relatively small investment firm did enough business to also have offices in Chicago and London. O'Neill found them to be receptive but not overly enthusiastic.

Thomas Lombard who had not been any further west

Polson family in Sweden with August, Jr. (top l.) and Frank (3rd from top l.) taken in 1883.   Polson Collection

5

than Chicago, was taken by Buckey's open manner and his stories of the wild west and the beauty and riches of the Grand Canyon. Buckey made several trips to New York and Chicago in the next several years trying to consolidate a deal with the company but it seemed most of his progress became limited to becoming a family friend of the Lombards.

Somehow Buckey had convinced enough small investors in the Williams area to come up with one thousand dollars to pay for a preliminary survey of the railroad. Crews completed the survey in 1894 and Buckey again went to see Thomas Lombard. This time he convinced Lombard of the need and reason for a personal inspection. Lombard made his first trip to the area in 1895 and O'Neill gave him and his party a royal tour of the region. He was not in any physical condition for such an arduous trip and tired easily. But in any case, he came away thoroughly impressed. Even so, on his return to New York no great rush for the company to get involved manifested itself. These were conservative men who were not very willing to risk a buck.

Although Lombard exhibited a considerable lack of definitive action, he had been convinced of this venture's sound potential. Also, the scenic beauty of the Grand Canyon captivated him. Still, his measured enthusiasm didn't put any money in the bank. In his plodding way, Lombard spent several years of futile effort trying to secure enough solid investors to make the railroad go. Lombard, Goode and Company formed the Tusayan Development Company to cover their several mining claims and provide for their development. This move provided an aura of respectability for the venture. Even by doing this, Lombard still failed to convince enough investors to part with their money.

O'Neill and Lombard then went to see E. P. Ripley, president of the Santa Fe Pacific Railroad, but they could not get him to invest the Santa Fe's money in this undertaking. In fact, Ripley considered Lombard, Goode and Company to be a fly-by-night organization and their project a "bluff" for years. He reiterated these sentiments time and again in his correspondence with subordinates. This opinion probably led to the demise of the original railroad project more than any other combination of factors.

Oddly enough, in spite of Ripley's opinion of Lombard, Goode and Company, Lowry Goode kept up a good rapport with Aldace F. Walker, the Chairman of the Boards for the AT&SFRy and Santa Fe Pacific. Cordial letters between the two usually expressed positive sentiments about the completion of the line. Apparently their relationship helped to keep the SF&GCRR

George U. Young, publisher and editor of the Williams News. He recovered only $500 of his large investment in the SF&GCRR.

Sullivant Collection

project moving forward as far as it concerned the AT&SF and SFP.

Apparently correspondence from O'Neill to Walker and Ripley proved a bit more persuasive and seemed to stir the railroad to action. Also, rich ore samples sent by O'Neill in 1897 had a strong bearing on the support given to the fledgling line by the Santa Fe. In a letter written 10 September 1897 on stationery from the Office of the Mayor of Prescott, O'Neill listed the following ore samples as being sent by express that day:

Two samples of asbestos
Sample of red ochre mineral paint
Sample of yellow ochre mineral paint
Sample of mica
Samples of lead and silver ore
Samples of gold bearing rock—sulphurets
Sample of copper ore

He continued on to say, "all of which are from the Grand Canyon of the Colorado, and all of which are found in large quantities. The copper ore I limited to one specimen as I understood from you in Flagstaff (O'Neill had met with them on 2 July) that you already had specimens of this rock. As this is a particularly fine sample though I thought it might interest you."

Buckey envisioned far more than mining when considering the benefits and potential of this railroad. He also foresaw the possibilities of tourist travel to the south rim. To this end he continued on in the same letter:

7

Surveyor W. H. Lockridge (c.) with his chainmen, J. Durane (r.) and J. Randall (l.) with the tools of their trade in 1900.   Moore Collection

I also send you a small map showing points in the Canyon which have heretofore received little attention, notably the very magnificent waterfalls, among them Rainbow [F]alls 1600 feet high, Mooney's Falls 265 feet and others. It also shows points of interest such as the Cathedral Cave 3200 feet deep, Echo Cliffs, the various named peaks of greatest prominence, etc., my idea being that if incorporated in the folders of the Santa Fe it would give the Canyon and [sic] individuality and attractiveness that it does not now possess for the ordinary traveller [sic] who regards it when looking at the map as merely a barren waste. As the Santa Fe has a kind of proprietary interest in the Canyon greater than anyone else, I think it should be willing of accepting the responsibility of sta[ge]ing for it. Really though the Canyon is a gold mine in the way of money-making for the Sa[n]ta Fe, and why it has never been recognized and worked as such I am at a loss to conceive.

Although O'Neill had an apparent need for either a new typewriter or secretary, this letter clearly showed his thoughts extended beyond mining interests when it came to the railroad.

In 1897 both Lombard and Goode made a survey trip of the proposed line. At that time they estimated a cost of ten thousand dollars per mile for construction. Of this figure O'Neill said to Walker, "...which is far in excess of what I had figured on."

Lombard and O'Neill kept plugging away. By 1897

Ledger sheet from the Anita Junction-Grand Canyon stage for October 1900.　　　　　　　　　　　Martin Buggeln Collection, NAU

they had secured enough investors, many of them small business-men from Williams and vicinity, to get things started. These included R. R. Coleman, Frank and August Polson, Max Salzman, George U. Young, James Walsh, J. M. Dennis Lumber Company,

Elmer Duffield (seated), an early   Frank and Florida Polson in their
Santa Fe Trainmaster, and family.   wedding picture, 1891.
Duffield Collection   Polson Collection

Arizona Central Bank and later the Saginaw and Manistee Lumber Company. The method of financing and the issuance of bonds became the major problems in putting the company into solvency. These remained to be haggled over until 1898.

Reports from a variety of sources indicated the investors from Williams put in somewhere around $200,000 toward the project. Although in 1897 the City of Williams boasted a railroad division headquarters, it nevertheless remained a relatively small town. For the businessmen of the community to make a financial commitment to the railroad of this magnitude speaks volumes as to its need and potential.

A big boost came when the 19th Territorial Legislature reestablished the expired tax incentives for building railroads within the Territory of Arizona. Finally convinced enough investment money existed, Lombard, Goode and Company incorporated the Santa Fe and Grand Canyon Railroad Company on 31 July 1897 with Lowry W. Goode as president.

Although it had taken several years the enterprise finally came together. In O'Neill's home town of Prescott the progress was duly reported in the 11 August 1897 issue of the *Arizona Weekly Journal-Miner.*

Plans have been perfected for a railroad to the Grand Canyon of the Colorado, and construction is to begin from a

10

point on the Santa Fe Pacific at Flagstaff or Williams. A tenth of the million dollar capital stock is already on hand, and the bonds of the line are being placed in the east. The enterprise is backed by Lombard, Goode & Co., of Chicago, and is under the management of Mayor O'Neill, of Prescott. The new line will be known as the Santa Fe and Grand Canyon Railroad and will be 72 miles in length, and will tap the canyon at the head of the Bright Angel trail. At that point is proposed the erection of a large hotel. Mr. O'Neill is now in the east in the interest of his railroad scheme.

The company also applied for and received a right of way across the Coconino National Forest Reserve. As recorded with the Coconino County Recorder it reads in part: "...Santa Fe and Grand Canyon Railroad Company running north to Lombard on the rim of the Grand Canyon of the Colorado River, a distance of 65 miles from Williams at the Santa Fe Pacific Railroad." Note the reference to "Lombard." Had this company completed the road to the Canyon, what is known as Grand Canyon Village today would have been known as Lombard, Arizona.

Now incorporated and apparently with sufficient funds to complete the project the SF&GCRR became a force to be reckoned with. Newspapers of the region carried stories of its progress and documented the competition between the various factions. The *Journal-Miner* reported the progress in the 13 October issue.

Mayor O'Neill has gone up to Williams and other points on the Santa Fe Pacific, to meet a party of eastern

Santa Fe Pacific locomotive number 49 and combination car number 204 at Anita Junction in 1900. Note water tank on flat car.
Coupland Collection, NAU

capitalists whome [sic] he has interested in the building of the new railroad to the Grand Canyon. The building of the road has been definitely settled, and the route is to be decided on. Williams and Flagstaff are lively competitors for it, but the former is said to have the preference, being more direct, and having in addition an easier grade and being less in distance. A force of men will be put to work inside of a week surveying and grading.

It took another month but during November and December of 1897 and January 1898 the survey, under the skilled hands of surveyor William Lockridge, was completed. Recorded at Coconino County is an affidavit of commencement of actual construction, a legality necessary to comply with the requirements of the Territorial Legislature tax exemptions. It states in part, "...between 24th day of February and 3rd day of March 1898 completed grading on 1650 feet of railroad from the Williams station east and northerly...moving 1050 6/10 cubic yards in earth excavation, earth embankment and loose rock." To any interested parties these milestones were assurances of the railroad's reality. However, the signing of far more import documents occurred in New York on the 16th of December, 1897.

A Joint Use Agreement between the Santa Fe Pacific Railroad and the Santa Fe & Grand Canyon Railroad for the station grounds in Williams signed and effective on the 16th gave the line needed access from the mainline to the northbound track. Probably the water delivery provisions at the rate of one dollar for every engine tank of thirty-five hundred gallons or less and water used for "other than engine purposes" at the rate of thirty cents per hundred (later amended to thousand) gallons were the most important conditions in this agreement. Also if water became unavailable in Williams, the SFP agreed to haul water from its wells at Bellemont or Ashfork at the rate of fifteen dollars per five thousand gallons. E. P. Ripley signed for the Santa Fe Pacific and Wm. O. O'Neill as the Vice President for the SF&GC.

A Joint Tariff Agreement effective 31 December 1897 brought legitimate business recognition from the rest of the railroad world. Upon completion of the line, "...freight and passengers shall be routed upon through joint tariff rates from all points upon any railroad owned or leased and operated by either of the Santa Fe Companies, to all points on the line of the Grand Canyon Company; and in a like manner all freight and passengers shall be routed upon through joint tariff rates from points on the Grand Canyon Railroad to all points on the aforesaid lines of the Santa Fe

Companies." Ripley signed as President for the Santa Fe Pacific Railroad, The Atchison, Topeka & Santa Fe Railway and Southern California Railway companies with O'Neill signing for the Santa Fe & Grand Canyon Railroad.

Certainly there would have been an article in the *Williams News* about the agreements but no surviving copies have been found. However, an article dated 24 December 1897 in an unidentified northern Arizona newspaper stated, "Word is received from Prescott that Buck[e]ly O'Neill has returned from New York, where he had been in the interest of his copper mines and smelter. Buck[e]ly says that both the smelter and Grand Canyon railroad are absolutely assured facts, as Lombard, Goode & Company are backing the ventures." Surely all would go well now. However, additional financial arrangements were yet to be made and these added to the delays.

When Buckey's project began to stall all of these situations must have been truly unsettling to the investors as no interest had been paid on their money and they were not the only ones interested in putting this railroad through. As early as 1892, *The Daily Star* of Tucson printed a story of "a force of thirteen teams" beginning work on the Flagstaff & Black Canyon Railroad to proceed from "...Cliff Spur, fourteen miles northeast of Flagstaff." It further stated, "The tourist and scientist will no longer be deterred from visiting the wonder of wonders on account of the inconvenience of stage or hack travel, but can ride in a palace car to [the] brink of the grand canyon of the Colorado."

Later, on 10 March 1896, articles of incorporation in the Territory of Arizona recorded the Globe, Flagstaff and Canyon Railroad "to Cameron Point on the Grand Canyon." This company had been previously incorporated as the Flagstaff and Canyon Railroad Company on 22 June 1895. Also, The Grand Canyon Railroad Company was incorporated on 16 June 1887 in Prescott with the intention of building a railroad from Seligman to the Canyon. Another company had secured from the 54th Congress a right-of-way from Flagstaff to the Grand Canyon on 8 June 1886.

Articles in the *Flagstaff Sun-Democrat* carried stories of the competition. The editor, in the 23 September 1897 issue, went so far as to state, "It is only a question of a few months till a railroad will be built from Flagstaff to the Grand Canyon, and then the Skylight City will have a substantial growth and a rapid increase in wealth and population. A smelter will be located here..." Certainly the people of Flagstaff could see the benefits of having the railroad run from their city to the south rim and the competition must have been intense. To this end the newspaper

Santa Fe railroad yards in 1902 with station and freight house up the line and downtown Williams to the left.　　　　　Samson Collection

articles continued. The 28 October issue carried this two line article, "When the Grand Canyon railroad is built, it will be built from Flagstaff." The investors of Williams had direct competition from their neighbors.

Even before the surveys had been completed it became obvious the route from Williams presented the best solution. Shorter by at least ten miles, the grade is not as steep as other proposals and Williams had already been designated as a division of the main east-west Santa Fe Pacific. With the final determinations made, and the agreements signed in December the Santa Fe and Grand Canyon Railroad from Williams to Anita and the Grand Canyon became reality. Still, for the following year the hassles continued with Ripley and others largely due to the railroad's lack of competent management.

Finally all of the components had come together. George Young must have been overjoyed when he printed the story in his *Williams News* stating roadbed construction commenced on 1 June 1899 with P. F. Randall as Chief Engineer of Construction. On 8 June, L. W. Goode and H. N. Goode incorporated The Canyon Construction Company in the Territory of Arizona "...to build railroads and all other accessories pertinent to railroads."

This news would have brought joy to the heart of Buckey O'Neill had he been there. After all of the effort, time and money he had expended, this was not to be. His adventuresome ways had finally caught up with him the previous year.

When Colonel Theodore Roosevelt organized his Regiment of Rough Riders at the onset of the Spanish American War, Buckey became the first to organize a troop to serve under him. Captain O'Neill put together a tough group of miners, cowboys and loggers from the Territory of Arizona into Troop A, First U.S. Volunteer Cavalry. These men served with great distinction in Cuba and particularly at Kettle Hill (usually reported as San Juan Hill), but not as cavalry. Their horses had been left behind in the United States due to lack of transport. While they operated as infantry preparatory to the attack of Kettle Hill, a Spanish sniper took aim at an officer walking up and down in full view giving encouragement to his men. The marksman adjusted his sights in the half light of dawn on the 1st of July 1898 and squeezed his trigger. Buckey O'Neill died doing what he did best—leading men into dangerous places and taking more risks than anyone else. He held the rank of Brevet Major at the time.

Buckey had survived many encounters with death at the hands of robbers and gunmen. A raging river drowned his horse but failed to claim him and he survived a leap from a moving train to capture an escaped prisoner. His luck ran out in Cuba and even his resourcefulness couldn't beat this one. He didn't live to see his efforts in behalf of the railroad come to realization. Certainly no one worked harder to bring it to northern Arizona and the south rim of the Canyon. If any one person is to be thanked or praised for making the Grand Canyon Railway a reality it is William Owen O'Neill.

Unissued Grand Canyon Railway Company preferred stock certificate number 50.

By the spring of 1899 all of the company's problems had not as yet been smoothed out. Much haggling still remained to be done with E. P. Ripley and the Santa Fe Pacific, successor to the Atlantic and Pacific in 1896. Also, another railroad company entered the arena that summer. This added aggravation came in the form of the Grand Canyon Railway Company of Arizona, being incorporated on 8 July 1899 to build north from Ash Fork. Fortunately for the SF&GCRR they ran into more difficulties with financing than Lombard, Goode and Company, even with Ripley's moral support.

Ripley had decided the Grand Canyon line would be added to the Santa Fe's roster of companies and he threw all of the legal roadblocks at his disposal into the path of Lombard, Goode & Company. Ripley, in no uncertain terms, stated to W. G. Nevin, his General Manager in Los Angeles, all dealings for rentals and purchases with the Santa Fe and Grand Canyon Railroad would be cash up front. Chief Engineer Randall of the SF&GCRR had asked for motive power, boarding trains, flat cars and rails as early as 15 August. But they were not immediately forthcoming and two more months of letters, telegrams and legal dealings passed back and forth between Williams, Los Angeles, Chicago and New York before final arrangements for equipment leases and material purchases from the Santa Fe Pacific could be made.

On 12 October 1899, Randall requested from Nevin the following:

Connection at the main line of the SFP with the SF&GC
1 engine, 19X26, 10 wheeler
18 box cars fitted for a boarding train
   1 kitchen
   1 commissary
   6 dining
   8 sleepers
   1 foreman
   1 trainmen [sic] and engineers
Coal, water, oil and waste for cars
1 engine additional and 15 flats for running material to the
   front

He figured at that time his crews had the capability of laying not more than 50 or 60 tons of rail per day and asked it be delivered along with fastenings at the rate requested on flat cars if possible. Randall had ordered 56 pound relay rail but the SFP shipped both 52 and 56 pound.

With final completion of the financial arrangements and Randall's request approved, Santa Fe Pacific locomotives 49 and 88 moved onto the Grand Canyon line for the first time. Number 49 later became 282 and the first regularly scheduled locomotive to the Grand Canyon. In June of 1900, SFP 51 replaced SFP 88. Both numbers 49 and 51 were of the 4-6-0 configuration and 88 was a 4-4-0. In the 1900 reorganization of motive power number 49 was renumbered to 282, 51 became 281 and 88 changed to 125. 49/282 and 51/281 had been built by Baldwin and 88/125 by New York.

Further agreements provided that the SFP supply water to the SF&GCRR for the locomotives at thirty cents per thousand gallons, necessary outfit and water cars be leased at the rate of $1.00 per day and one coach at the rate of $2.50 and car SFP 204 at $1.50 per day. This last combination car made the initial run on 17 September with number 282 and it remained in passenger service on the line for many years.

And so the initial business had been completed. The Santa Fe and Grand Canyon Railroad now had its motive power and rolling stock on lease and the materials needed to complete track to the mines and the rim. At what cost? The contract guaranteed them a price of 56 pound relay rail and fastenings at $25.00 per ton plus shipping at one cent per ton per mile. But there was a catch and it dictated that supplies and services be paid for in SF&GC gold bonds to Santa Fe at the rate of sixty cents on the dollar. In effect, cost of the rail and fastenings now became $41.266 per ton. As it turned out, with intent by Ripley and foolishness on the part of Lombard and Goode, this literally cut the heart out of the company.

Business done with various supply companies also used bonds for payment. For instance, the company issued forty shares of common stock to purchase three carloads of track spikes from the Richmond Standard Steel Spike & Iron Company of Richmond, Virginia. As the bonds became worth less and less these companies became part of a long list of creditors left holding the bag.

Lombard and Goode never listed these bonds on the stock exchange and could redeem them only with the Santa Fe Pacific. Later on, Ripley cut the value to forty cents and then again to ten cents on the dollar. At this rate it did not take too long before the Santa Fe and Grand Canyon found themselves in serious financial condition.

Added to this, lack of water rendered the Anita Copper Company's smelter inoperable. Built at the east end of

Williams it depended on the Santa Fe dam for water and without water it was useless. Just as Lombard, Goode & Company expected to go into operation, they received notification from the AT&SF that the Santa Fe dam had partially "washed out" and the remaining water had to go to their own railroad and the town of Williams. The AT&SF would not honor their contract. Certainly the Santa Fe found it most convenient that only enough water had been lost to "honorably" disallow water use by the smelter but enough remained for them and the town of Williams to operate. Speculation was rife as to the involvement of the railroad company in the washout.

Due to the damaged dam, water became a scarce and expensive commodity and a concern to all. When Mr. McFarland of the Tusayan Company took his family to Williams for an inspection visit a servant accompanied them. One morning he came to Mrs. McFarland and asked, "What we goin' to do about that lady next door? She borrowed a whole bucket of water last week and ain't never said nothing about bringing it back!" This must have been how Lombard, Goode & Company and their investors began to feel.

In spite of these financial difficulties, railroad construction pushed north to Anita Junction, 45 miles north of Williams. From here the 2.87 mile spur to Anita Camp, the mining destination of the railroad, joined the main line. Anita Junction (later Anita), Anita Camp and the Anita Mines all received their names after Thomas Lombard's daughter. On 15 March 1900 the Santa Fe and Grand Canyon Railroad opened up for operations.

Copper ore finally came out of the mines and the railroad carried it to Williams. Passenger service also came into being. Tourists could now board the train in Williams and travel the 45 miles north to Anita Junction in comfort and with speed. Here they would have to board stage coaches for the remaining twenty mile trip to the Canyon. The trip had been cut from three days to one of five and a half hours as the road north from Anita Junction usually remained in good condition.

A time card published in the *Williams News* of 22 June 1901 showed train number 10 leaving Williams for Anita Junction at 12:30 PM via Red Lake, Prado, Valle and Willaha. From there the stage left at 3:00 PM with arrival at the Grand Canyon via Anita and Coconino at 6:00 PM. This return trip by stage left the Grand Canyon at 1:30 PM to meet the train at Anita Junction for a 4:00 PM departure to Williams with scheduled arrival at 6:30 PM. Most likely this time table had been followed from the beginning of service.

The Santa Fe masonry dam south of Williams. Primary source of water for the railroad and the town.   Baumgartner-Leonard Collection

What a relief these events must have brought to all parties involved. It does not take much imagination to hear the toasts and cheers offered at Anita, Williams, New York and Chicago. In spite of Ripley's maneuvering they had succeeded!

With passenger service on the Santa Fe and Grand Canyon Railroad finally a reality, Lombard, Goode & Company then turned their energies to the completion of the railroad to the rim. They found reality to be a two edged sword because their remaining capital would allow them to complete only another 8.63 miles. Joy expressed at the completion of the line to Anita must have been short lived. Surely it didn't require a genius to figure out the SF&GC was in terrible financial shape.

The "water shortage" caused the smelter to remain inoperable and company officials began to consider the use of alternative facilities. However, transportation costs of ore to smelters in other parts of the Arizona Territory would eat into any profits derived from the mines. Passenger revenues could not even begin to cover the costs of operation. Bonds used to purchase materials from the Santa Fe Pacific continued to be undercut by Ripley and investors never received any interest. To top it all off, the realization finally struck home that enough ore to make a profit on such a large investment did not exist. Perhaps the Spanish sniper who killed Buckey O'Neill spared him the pain he would have experienced at the demise of the fruits of his labors.

Buckey can be labeled many things but failure has never been one of them. Only his selection of business partners could be brought into question. Possibly the SF&GCRR's history might have been different had that sniper just flinched a little bit.

The last straws began to fall in August of 1900. Several Mechanic's and Merchant's Liens were filed against the railroad. R. R. Coleman, one of the contractors, filed the largest claim for $28,435.48 in wages (at $1.75 to $2.00 per day) owed his workmen and another $30,000 in supplies and materials. With no cash to pay off the liens and the outstanding bonds held by other creditors only one thing could be done. On 5 September 1900 the company went into receivership. The reorganization committee held title to the properties of the SF&GCRR until 15 August 1901. Interestingly, members of this committee, Judge Edward D. Kenna, Byron L. Smith and James H. Eckels, all served as board members or worked for the Santa Fe.

The Santa Fe Pacific held the largest amount of bonds totaling $324,000. In addition, they advanced $200,000 to the reorganization committee for the purchase of the road, to settle claims and to complete construction of the railroad. Of this $150,000 went to pay off the small investors. But this amount didn't even begin to cover the losses of these individuals who had put their businesses and private fortunes in hock for the grand venture. The smaller investors of Williams received only a percentage and all lost about ninety percent of their original investment. So much for the free enterprise of "small" investors. For what amounted to a highly discounted $324,000 in bonds and a $200,000 cash outlay, the Santa Fe Pacific Railroad (actually the parent company The Atchison, Topeka & Santa Fe Railway) became owner of a nearly completed railroad from Williams to the Grand Canyon.

Final sale on 20 July 1901 and title transfer on 15 August completed the transaction. An article in the *Williams News* of 22 June stated the Santa Fe bought out the Grand Canyon Railroad Company from Lombard, Goode and Company and other minor investors for $150,000 on 8 June. Max Salzman managed to recover $12,150 (much of which came from a Merchant's Lien due on supplies sold to the railroad) but George Young's share only came to five hundred dollars. The Santa Fe paid out another $50,000 to satisfy a variety of claims and liens for goods and wages.

Complete financial control of the new railroad came with the transfer of 12,053 shares of capital stock to the reorganization committee between 19 September 1901 and 1 March 1902. Lowry Goode continued to assist the Santa Fe in the liquidation of

Santa Fe Route
TIME TABLE.

CORRECTED TO DECEM-
BER 27, 1900

SF&GCRR time card dated March, 1900 and Santa Fe time table dated December, 1900 from the *Williams News.*

privately held shares in the Santa Fe and Grand Canyon Railroad until 1911. In correspondence he repeatedly referred to the Grand Canyon line as "our little road" and commented how close he held it in his heart.

In reality one wonders with what affection he held the line. Lowry Goode had his fingers in so many corporations it must have been a real trick to keep track of his involvements. In addition to the Grand Canyon line he held the presidency for two other railroads no longer with us today. The Cairo & Norfolk and the Cairo and Tennessee River Railroad Companies disappeared into history much the same as the SF&GCRR. Along with these and a myriad of companies, which were speculative almost without exception, he held officerships which ranged from treasurer to president. Coincidentally, all of these companies had offices at 111 Broadway in New York City. For a short time in 1902 he held thirty shares of common stock in The Grand Canyon Railway.

Another interesting stockholder in the new company, Mrs. Rose E. Lombard, held ten shares of common stock from 1902 to 1904. Considering her opinion of E. P. Ripley and the heartache this venture had caused her husband this was indeed a firm testimony for the future of The Grand Canyon Railway.

On 10 August the Santa Fe incorporated The Grand Canyon Railway Company in the Territory of Arizona. In April of 1902 the company went public with issues of capital stock valued at $1,455,000 and paying five percent interest. Shares of preferred stock amounting to $250,000 and $1,205,000 in common stock went on the market at one hundred dollars per share. Through ownership of a majority of the outstanding capital stock, The Atchison, Topeka and Santa Fe Railway Company held control until sale of the railroad to Railroad Resources, Inc. in 1984 and then again to the Grand Canyon Railway company in 1988.

Operations continued and passenger revenues remained a part of this line while in receivership. As best as can be determined in the record, the schedule printed previously was maintained with little or no interruption of service.

Although George Young lost his shirt in the aborted SF&GCRR venture he still managed to print the applicable news of the GCRy as it occurred—much like a proud parent. One such article appeared in the 23 February 1901 issue of the *Williams News*. It stated in part, "...first double header left for the Grand Canyon [Anita Junction] on February 21, 1901, composed of engines 49 and 610 with three special cars from the New York Central Railroad, a dining car from the Southwest Limited and one baggage car." Although he later acted as a director of the new company for a time, Mr. Young's losses amounted to $75,000 and he needed to recoup. On 3 August 1901 he sold the *Williams News* to Messrs. C. A. Neal and L. H. Dawley. This done he left for Prescott to involve himself in mining and politics.

Times were tough. People were tough. They might be down but they weren't out. Neither was the Grand Canyon Railway. Its history started for the second time.

THE MINES

No less than thirty one mining companies incorporated in Coconino County between the years 1891 (when it became separate from Yavapai County) and 1904. The number of separate mining claims is astronomical. A great many of these are in the Francis or Grand Canyon Mining District adjacent to the Grand Canyon Railway. Some of these claims and corporations provided justification for the railroad and others used the railroad to haul ore once it became established. Most were not worth the time and effort taken to record them and many were out-and-out investment scams.

In the Territory of Arizona during the 1880s and 1890s, mining was a prime draw for investment and promotion. Miners and promoters recorded claims all over the territory from north to south and from east to west. Companies formed anywhere promoters thought they could raise money for their scams and not necessarily just in Arizona. An article in the distant *Tombstone Weekly Prospector* of 23 October 1890 listed The Grand Canyon Mining Company as having inaugurated business in San Diego "...to prospect the Grand Canyon of the Colorado for gold, between Lee's Ferry and the Virgin River."

Hundreds of prospectors poked around any place active work had not begun. Some of these prospectors held prominent positions in the Territory. Buckey O'Neill, one of those individuals who couldn't sit still for very long and one of the more active men in the Francis District, prospected and staked his

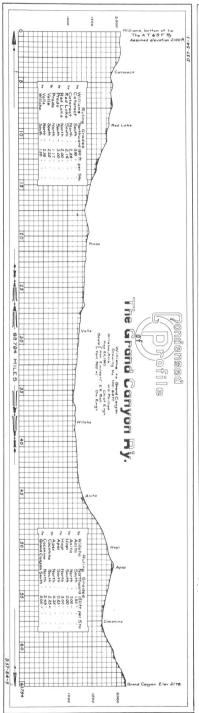

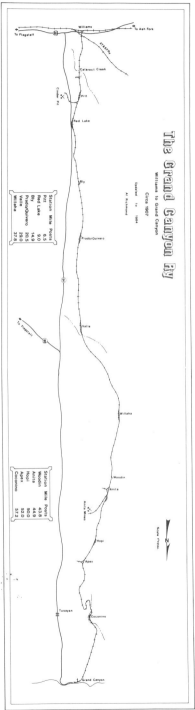

The Grand Canyon Ry

Williams to Grand Canyon

Circa 1907

Updated to 1984

Al. Richmond

Station	Mile Posts
Pitt	6.5
Red Lake	9.0
Bly	14.9
Prado/Quivero	20.5
Valle	29.0
Willaha	37.8

Station	Mile Posts
Woodin	43.8
Anita	44.9
Hopi	50.0
Apex	52.0
Coconino	57.2

claims. As he and his friends combed the region for signs of "color," they became more and more convinced money could be made here. But they knew as well as anyone else ore is worthless if it can't be gotten out of the ground and processed for a reasonable cost.

Wagons did not provide an answer to the problem but a railroad certainly did. A railroad needed to be built in to the claims and this required money. More money than available in the Territory. Several years passed before these people had an answer to their dilemma.

A knowledge of the terrain and geology of the area is important to understand why prospectors and engineers believed the Francis District held great riches and why it only made limited returns for the efforts expended. Starting at Williams at an elevation of 6700 feet above sea level and moving north along the railroad the terrain is rolling with shallow cuts for streams. Much of the area forms the drainage for Cataract Creek which flows through the Havasupai Reservation and on into the Colorado River. The surface is dotted with volcanic cinder cones which provided ballast for the roadbed in later years. Vegetation ranges from a variety of grasses grading into juniper and pinyon pine and denser Ponderosa pine. Just north of Williams the railroad climbs up out of town through a beautiful stand of tall Ponderosa pines and grades into a pinyon-juniper environment after milepost (MP) 4 with rolling hills and valleys.

North of MP 19 the terrain becomes primarily high desert. The profile is one of low rolling hills and wide plains that drop to a low point of 5800 feet. The vegetation ranges from many varieties of grasses through cliffrose, chamiza and big sage brushes into varying densities of juniper and pinyon pine.

Climbing up the grade north of MP 45, outcrops of limestone become readily apparent. Off to the east Red Butte is visible in the distance with its remnant Moenkopi Formation capped by basalts. Moenkopi sandstone, to the same depth as Red Butte, at one time covered all of the area visible from the railway. Almost all of this material has since eroded away. Remnant Moenkopi is quite apparent in the reddish soils of the region. Vegetation becomes denser as the Canyon is approached. Grasses of several varieties along with the same varieties of brush grade into pinyon-juniper and on into the denser stands of tall Ponderosa pines north of MP 51.

No great vegetation changes are evidenced with the dips and rises through Coconino Wash until at 6800 feet the south rim of the Grand Canyon is reached. Here some scrub oaks make their appearance. At the rim the drop off of 5000 feet to the

Sorting copper ore for loading onto burros. Some miners transported ore to the nearest railroad siding in this manner. Sullivant Collection

Colorado River gives a cross section view of the terrain traveled from Williams, revealing several sedimentary layers of different materials and origins. Many different episodes of deposition and wearing away of marine and wind blown sediments left a layer cake effect. Upper layers of this cake provide the setting for most of the mines of this area and it is the setting for the mines that brought the railroad to this region.

Several small, scattered copper deposits occur in these strata of the Grand Canyon Mining District. These are found in breccia (pronounced breshia) pipes of the south rim and in the areas south to about MP 37. Breccia pipes are mostly cylindrical, vertical structures composed of angular and frequently rounded rock fragments enclosed in a matrix of comminuted rock paste or subsequently introduced material. In short, it is a vertical or horizontal tube in the host rock filled with material which originated at another location.

The breccia pipes on the south rim extend through the uppermost layers known as the Kaibab Limestone, the Toroweap Formation, Coconino Sandstone and the Hermit Shale. In the area of the Anita Mines it is unknown if the pipes extend below the Toroweap Formation as they have not been probed any deeper.

Several theories have been advanced on the origin of the breccia pipes in this area. At the rim it is thought a cavern collapse scenario took place. This is a situation whereby the roof of a cavern, formed when the underlaying limestone is dissolved

26

out by surface water, collapses and the cavern is filled in by overlying sediments. In the area of the Anita Mines the story appears to be different. Present thinking is the removal of limestone and carbonate cements by rising, reactive hydrothermal (hot liquid) solutions disintegrated the overlying rock layers and generated the collapse. These hydrothermal solutions, flowing into the sediments within the pipes, transported and deposited the minerals to be mined centuries later.

Whatever the scenario of deposition, the result is highly concentrated ore bodies which are usually very limited in their content. Concentrations of copper ore are so high in some breccias that it assayed out at sixty-five percent in the early 1900s. Imagine what riches had been expected from these mines when five percent ore is considered very good. Many copper mines in Arizona made their fortunes on five percent or less ore.

The deepest shaft at the primary Anita claim only went to 530 feet before it pinched out. This claim provided what might well be the richest assay of copper ore in Arizona history due to its concentration. The deepest and most productive mine in the Francis District is the Orphan Mine on the south rim of the Canyon. A cable tramway ran down the canyon wall to the Supai Formation where a horizontal drift (tunnel) into the breccia pipe provided the means of ore removal to the surface. When the tramway became hard to maintain the company later updated the mine with a 1600 foot deep vertical shaft to a 1400 foot cross cut.

Ladders to the Sometime mine in the Grand Canyon.

Sullivant Collection

27

The headframe for the mine still stands on the rim to the west of the Powell Memorial.

Actually situated on the rim of the Canyon, the Orphan Mine by far had the most diverse mineral content of the mines in the district. Originally a copper claim, it closed down in 1969 after mining uranium, its most profitable ore. Copper showed up in many forms with uranium being of the U308 variety. Other ores mined profitably were antimony, barite, cobalt, calcite, gold, iron, lead, molybdenom, silver and zinc. All-in-all a total of thirty-three different minerals are known in the Orphan claim.

At the Anita and Copper Queen mines to the south the findings are a bit more conservative. Their ores are primarily copper bearing with dolomite, germanium, goethite, gold, hematite, silver and U308 in trace or unprofitable amounts. Uranium has been found in only a few of the claims. To exploit these resources in the early 1900s miners used every conceivable method known with the possible exception of hydraulic mining. Some commonly practiced "high grading" in the claims where small, rich concentrations were found. This process required breaking of cobbles by hand with a hammer on an anvil. A piece of railroad track made the usual anvil in this district. For the amount of work involved this is a most unprofitable means of mining but it became a routine technique in the region during the Depression years. Other methods included the pick and shovel in

Rotting ties are all that remain of the Anita Spur.

Mine tunnel opening at the Anita mines.

Remains of ore loading ramp at Anita constructed in 1918 for William Lockridge by the AT&SFRy.

near-surface stopes or use of bulldozers to break up the material for loading.

An asbestos mine deep in the Canyon and across the river had to be mined by hand tools. John Hance and his men ferried the ore across the river, transported it to the south rim by burro and then loaded it into hopper cars on the railroad. This mine produced some of the longest asbestos fibers known. Fibers from the Hance mine reached lengths in excess of four inches where the standard today is around one quarter inch. These fibers found their way to theaters around the world for use in fire-proof curtains.

As the word spread in the early 1890s about the rich copper ore finds in the Francis District, prospectors, promoters, speculators and flim-flam men flooded the area. Mining companies formed overnight with nothing more to show than an address. They all found out nothing could be done without a way to get the ore to a smelter cheaply. This situation forced the mines in operation to pack the ore out on burros or mules or haul it in wagons to a pick up point on the main line of the A&P, or later on, the AT&SF. Shipping costs to smelters quickly wiped out any profits.

After Buckey O'Neill finally convinced Thomas Lombard of the fortunes to be made simply by building a railroad from Williams up to what became Anita, and hauling out the ore, the claims had to be surveyed and consolidated. For this task

O'Neill chose the man who earned a reputation as the most qualified and skilled surveyor in the region. William Lockridge surveyed most of the claims in the Francis District. Having surveyed much of the northern Arizona Territory he became very familiar with the region and had also filed some claims of his own. Especially for the time and with the relatively unsophisticated instruments available, Lockridge did such thorough work that his surveys have not been able to be improved upon and are still on file at the Coconino County Recorder's Office.

Lockridge also picked up some of the abandoned claims after the Santa Fe and Grand Canyon Railroad went out of business. He and Buckey O'Neill and later a Mr. H. K. MacDonald of Williams (in reality, Chicago), had filed most of the original claims for Lombard, Goode and Company. Most of these became incorporated into the Anita Consolidated Copper Company on 23 November 1899.

A majority of the claims represent original filings but many others had been purchased from miners who did not have enough money to work their claims. The Anita company bought up most of these claims in 1899. Even after the railroad declared bankruptcy active acquisition and working of these claims continued on up until 1905 when the Anita Copper Company finally abandoned any hopes of large scale mining of the region around Anita. Mining after this time drifted into small scale operations on an individual basis. Some of these original claims are being explored today with the hopes of finding sizeable uranium deposits.

Nuclear fuels companies are presently engaged in uranium mining on the north rim of the Canyon with extensive exploration taking place on the south rim region. At this time, a mining company is fighting environmentalists, the Havasupai Indian Tribe and concerned citizens over such a mine. Their plan is to establish a large scale operation east of the old Anita claims a few miles to the east of State Road 64 and only thirteen miles from the south rim of the Canyon.

This mine is located on the headwaters of Red Horse Wash which flows directly into Cataract Creek, through the Havasupai Reservation and on into the Colorado River. If one doubts the possibilities of Mother Nature having the upper hand in this region please consider that a single thunderstorm in 1916 on these same drainages destroyed three bridges, wrecked a train and killed the fireman. Also consider the radioactive pollution disaster of the Rio Puerco, Little Colorado River and the Colorado River caused by failure of the waste pond dam at the Church Rock

Remains of the smelter site at the Anita mines.

mine in New Mexico after a thunderstorm in 1979. The effects of this disaster will be felt for many generations. Hopefully we have seen the last of the uranium mines in the Francis District.

With the railroad in operation the Anita Copper Company built a smelter in Williams at the east end of town in anticipation of the riches believed to be forthcoming from the Anita area mines and those in the Grand Canyon. The *Williams News* frequently mentioned test runs of ore and the smelter finally became operational sometime in late 1901 or early 1902. It was an exercise in futility. Due to loss of water under highly suspect circumstances it never reached full production.

After the collapse of the SF&GCRR the Anita Copper Company remained in business and tried to recoup some of the losses sustained in the railroad failure. The company tried a new "George Process," named after its inventor, and made test runs of the smelter but not enough ore existed to make continued operations profitable in Williams. With the minimal amounts of ore available from the Anita mines transportation costs on the railroad became prohibitive. For all practical purposes, as long as the smelter remained in Williams it never became operational although it had the capability of processing ore.

The *Williams News* duly reported the mining news and the hopes and despair of the times. On 26 December 1903 a long editorial on the lack of work in the Francis mining district told of the plight faced by local area miners. "Most claim holders do not have the money to work the claims. They are just holding on waiting for someone else to strike it big and bring them a good price for their claim."

A major article in the weekly of 6 February 1904 gave a more promising outlook. The story promised expansion of the Anita Copper Company with present work going on at three hundred and expectations for the shaft to reach down to one thousand feet. In evidence for this expansion it further mentioned the "...smelter, boilers and engine sent to mine to furnish power." The writer boosted the outlook for future prosperity in the Francis District with a notation "Hance Asbestos Company to begin on a large scale and Canyon Copper Company will also increase."

An even longer article the following week on 13 February noted "...the smelter in Williams has been shut down...the ore was not rich enough to pay for transportation and smelter charges." Who or what was to be believed in these conflicting stories? Prospectors and miners are eternal optimists but stories such as these must have really kept those people of the Francis District in a quandary.

Such news did not totally dismay the miners at Anita. If Mohammed could not go to the mountain profitably then they would bring the mountain to Mohammed. An article in the issue of 14 May stated, "Materials [boilers and firebrick] from the Williams smelter was loaded in cars ready to go to Anita." Remnants of the firebrick and slag can still be found at Anita today. The smelter must have been packed up and sent on very

Collapsed head frame over the primary 530 foot deep shaft at the Anita mine.

short notice as an article in *The Boston Globe* dated 4 June commented on a trip made by a Col. J. T. Small of Lewiston, Maine to the mines described

>...a region rich in mineral deposits that may be mined at a small outlay on account of the formations so near the surface. The most promising properties in that wealthy district, in my opinion, after an examination covering 12 days, are the claims of the Anita Copper Company. These mines are located 15 miles south of the rim of the grand canyon [sic] on the new tourist railroad to the canyon, the *Santa Fe and Grand Canyon* branch of the Santa Fe railroad. The railroad runs right to the mine and from there south 47 miles to Williams, where the company's smelter is located. [Italics added]

As the article stated, Col. Small just returned from Arizona on 2 June, and it is interesting to consider that his train must have been leaving Williams just about the time the Anita Copper Company packed up its smelter. If he truly made an independent survey he must have been given a very selective tour and not allowed to read the local papers as he further stated in his article,

>On the 33 Anita claims most of the work has been done in open cuts so you can see the rich strata near the

Lockridge cabin, built in 1905, at the Emerald mine, one of the original Anita claims.

surface. The cuts run from 15 to 40 feet deep. They have one shaft in the North Star mine which is down to 300 feet, and they propose to continue sinking this shaft and to run drifts from the same. I was amazed at the ore I picked up. I found that the ore runs from 8 to 40 percent copper, and in many instances assays as high as 60 percent.

The Anita mines are most advantageously located with their 700 acres right on the railroad. Ore is loaded on cars at the mine and delivered at the company's smelter at Williams. The smelter is a first class plant, and the company owns 160 acres at Williams. On the whole I never saw any mining proposition that seems to have such great possibilities as the Anita.

One must wonder at the qualifications of Col. Small to make such a survey. Possibly he was a shill for the company in attempts to secure additional eastern funding for the project or the failing company was merely using him. These thoughts come to mind if consideration of his reference to the "Santa Fe and Grand Canyon branch" has any bearing on his connections. Since 1901 the line had been The Grand Canyon Railway. Lowry Goode was the president of the SF&GCRR when it failed and at the time of the article president of the Anita Copper Company. He continued for many years to refer to that line as his "little line" and it would be easy to believe his influence on Col. Small could have produced this

Open seam mining scar on one of the Copper Queen claims. The fossil mammal finds occurred in a site such as this.

Headquarters shack for the Copper Queen claims which are south of the Anita claims.

story. If he had this much influence it is not hard to believe Small actually worked for Goode and wrote as directed.

Things went reasonably well for a short period of time for in the *Williams News* publication of 26 November the following notation appeared: "The Anita mine is down to 540 feet in hard sandstone." However, this is as deep as the mine would get. On 18 May 1905 the newspaper reported that work at the Anita Copper Company had stopped and all men laid off pending settlement of attachment proceedings.

It was all over.

Although large scale mining of the Anita claims had come to a halt the effects and evidence of their tenure have been apparent for a long time. The scars upon the landscape are still very much present and if one takes the time to look through the mining records of the Coconino County Recorder all of the names of the claims can be found.

If ever such a thing existed as the romance of mining it had to be expressed in the names of the claims. The romance certainly had nothing to do with the hard work required to wrestle meager sums from tons of rock and spending many hours digging in a damp hole in the ground just does not seem to spark much excitement. But there must be something to it for many songs have been written about such doings and their dangers. Other than the articles in the *Williams News* and the names of the claims in the Coconino County Recorder's books, not much has survived in print about the mines of this region.

The romantic names of claims come from every source imaginable. Probably many have originated in the fuzzy mind of a prospector on a drunken toot celebrating a happy find. Most come from either the nostalgic remembrance of friends, relatives, business partners or locations of claims. Others are just plain fanciful. Some of the claims in the Francis district show a bit of tradition, imagination and whimsy.

Hope of good things to come probably inspired the Champion, Lucky Run and Buster claims. Home, family, friends or business associates most likely provided the sources of Anita (Lombard's daughter), Ethel, Ruby, Richmond and the Highland Mary. Obviously location determined the names for the Copper Hill, Hillside Mine, North End, Cold Spring and the Log Cabin. Possibly the best names came from the fancy of the miner and these resulted in the Copper Prince, Copper Queen, Copper King, Anita Queen, East View, Afterthought, Magician, Wizard, Commodore Dewey, North Star, Eastern Star, Willow, Alder, Tel Star, Golden Eagle, Hockataia, and the Grand View. With such wonderful names these claims deserved a better fate.

Also, the mines have been well documented in one area not generally associated with a profit motive. Vertebrate paleontology is the study of fossil animal remains. Normally this might not provide a dollar profit but it can certainly produce a handsome profit in knowledge of the previous occupants and environments of the world in which we live. It came as a pleasant surprise to the paleontological scholars of the world when in 1901 Doctor B. C. Bickell of the National Museum (Smithsonian) made an important mammal fossil find in the Copper Queen claims. A subsequent visit in 1904 by Doctor Barnum Brown, also of the National Museum, produced even more fossils.

Miners discovered the fossils in a fracture of the carboniferous (Kaibab) limestone. A deposit of sand seven or eight feet thick, which was lying on the bottom of the cave or fissure, buried and helped preserve the fossil remains. Although broken up, the bones remained in a good state of preservation. As the Kaibab is of marine origin, these fossil remains of terrestrial mammals make a unique collection. More importantly, this significant find listed eight previously unknown species. All of these specimens are now located at the National Museum in Washington, D. C.

Location of the fossils in a Permian age strata produced another problem. The Permian is a geologic time before mammals existed. The clue, "buried in a deposit of sand," gives rise

Families who settled at Anita built a fine, small communmity of houses and a school. The owners of this house moved it to Williams when they could no longer make a living at Anita.

to the reasonable conclusion of this being a subsidence area (the claim was a suspected breccia pipe prospect site) and it filled in by stream action or eolian (wind blown) deposits. The site could have been a depression with water which trapped the animals as they came to drink. Actual site location is presently not possible so the paleoenvironment is yet to be determined. Animal remains taken from the site include: badger, camel (llama), rabbits, woodchuck, packrat, pocket gopher, wolf, pronghorn, peccary and squirrel. Not a bad haul for an "unprofitable" claim.

All was not really a waste at Anita. A fine community of about twenty families grew up there with a section and bunk-house for the railroad and a livestock shipping point for the ranchers. The mines of the area used the ramp located by the stockyards to load their ore into cars for shipment on the railroad. A small school district started and teachers taught lessons to children of the area in a one room converted boxcar. It later grew into a nice school house complete with a small bell tower. The cause has escaped us but in 1928 it burned down and another boxcar replaced it in 1929. Apparently the school started about 1920 but this cannot be determined with certainty because the records of the 7th district prior to 1925 and after 1937 have been lost. It lasted into the early 1940s.

Residents built several nice houses there and a small store with a post office. Bill Lockridge's wife Grace served as postmaster for its duration from 17 August 1914 to 31 August

1918. The Anita-Moqui District Forest Service Station headquartered here prior to being relocated in Tusayan. None of these buildings remain at Anita. Some were moved to Williams in the 1950s and the rest dismantled.

On 23 April 1969 the last ore train with its load of uranium from the Orphan mine bound for New Mexico left the siding at milepost 63 in the Grand Canyon National Park behind locomotives 735, 1339 and 1317. As he sounded the horn, pushed the throttle forward and began to pick up speed one wonders if engineer N. S. McLean gave thought to the closing of an era. Did he, or anyone else there realize that with this train load the purpose which brought the railroad to the rim of the Grand Canyon no longer existed? Maybe conductor D. G. Jennings mused over the work and dreams of the people of the Anita Mines as the train drifted down the grade to MP 45 and what had been Anita Junction. Certainly it was worth at least a parting thought.

3

COMPLETION & REBUILDING

In 1901 The Grand Canyon Railway commenced operations legally as a new and separate company but in reality the Atchison, Topeka and Santa Fe Railway Company retained control. E. P. Ripley and the Santa Fe Board of Directors now had what they wanted—a railroad to the rim of the Grand Canyon. The process of acquisition entailed considerable legal maneuvering, luck and poor business management on the part of Lombard, Goode and Company over a period of several years but now the Santa Fe owned it outright.

What did they actually have? All of the right-of-way, sidings, passing track and spurs amounting to 63.81 miles of main line, with 53.62 miles in service and the remainder yet to be built, 13.232 miles of yard tracks and sidings, and 2.87 miles of spur track to the Anita Mines. In reality they acquired a second-class road because the Santa Fe and Grand Canyon people had been in a hurry and cut a few too many corners.

The inherited road bed could hardly be considered anything more than a logging dirt track with ties laid on the grade without ballast in many places and dirt ballast on the rest. Before operations could continue safely the new Grand Canyon Railway company began improvements and classified them as "additions and betterments." Projects such as the widening of embankments, ballasting the entire line and building passing tracks (sidings) received the highest priorities. Ripley planned for the building of hotels, curio shops, depots and other facilities but these projects

Engine 282 with the first passenger train from Williams to the Grand
Canyon.   National Park Service

waited until completion of the right-of-way construction. Other
facilities included the section and bunk houses, water towers and
cisterns at the stations along the line. Much work needed to be
done.

Completion of the main line to the rim of the Grand
Canyon topped the list of Santa Fe priorities. With the railroad in
place they could begin to develop and make a return on their
investment. Anticipation in Williams ran high as an item in the
13 July 1901 issue of the *Williams News* indicated; "B. Lantry
Sons, so it is rumored, will complete the canyon railroad shortly
almost in the twinkling of an eye." A story in the 27 July issue
clearly showed they wasted no time. "Work is progressing rapidly
on the completion of the Grand Canyon Railway. Over one
hundred teams and all the men possible to secure are working for
B. Lantry & Sons of Strong City, Kansas, who are rushing the work
to completion as fast as possible."

Another article in the edition of 14 September gave
testimony that Lantry's crews lived up to their press. "On Wednesday [11 Sep] of this week the laying of steel was finished. Ballasting and putting in the necessary "Y" at the terminal yet
remains to be done. The first train is due to be run by next Tuesday
[17 Sep]." And certainly it did, for the issue of 21 September gave
the following account: "The first regular train to cover the entire
distance from Williams to the Grand Canyon made the trip on last

Tuesday [17 Sep]. The road bed is in first class condition and a good rate of speed is maintained the entire length of the line. The schedule was: Williams to the Grand Canyon at 7:00PM-10:00PM; Grand Canyon to Williams at 8:30AM-11:20AM."

Still, there is disagreement about the date and whether this train made the trip as a passenger or freight consist. In any event the first scheduled train to the Grand Canyon left on 17 September 1901, but subsequent accounts have left confusing evidence for both the date and consist. The classic photo, which appeared in *The Santa Fe Magazine* of December 1929, shows locomotive 282, a ten wheeler 4-6-0 of the 281 class, and a consist of three water cars and a combination passenger/baggage car with engineer Harry Schlee at the controls and conductor Less Waddlee in charge. The caption reads in part: "FIRST TRAIN TO CARRY PASSENGERS TO THE GRAND CANYON OF ARIZONA. The party shown in this photograph left Williams, Ariz. on September 18, 1901, and took the last stage coach from the end of the railway to the cañon, some eight miles distant."

This photograph was dated 20 September when it appeared in a 1930 *Coconino Sun* story. If this date is correct it could reasonably mean the passengers stayed over the night of 19 September and returned to Williams the morning of 20 September but this is not likely. Additionally, the list of people in the photograph in the *Sun* story includes at least one individual who could not possibly have been there. Emery Kolb did not arrive at the Canyon until October, 1902. To compound the situation, other sources quoted as late as 1986 have given a date of 16 September. It would be nice to nail the date down exactly but records of Santa Fe train movements prior to 1930 are fragmentary at best and in most cases, non-existent.

It would seem more prudent to give credibility to the newspaper stories printed at the time of occurrence and not subsequent articles written at least twenty-eight years later. The idea of the train on 17 September being a freight is just that, an idea. No evidence exists which shows the train as a freight consist. Until hard evidence which proves a date other than as given in the *Williams News* stories surfaces, 17 September 1901 appears to be the most logical choice for the first scheduled passenger train from Williams to the Grand Canyon.

Effective with Time Table No. 2 on 1 October 1901, train No. 10 left Williams at 7:00PM and arrived at the Grand Canyon at 10:00PM. The return was by train No. 11 leaving at 9:00AM and arriving at 11:50AM in Williams.

Although this event represented big news to the

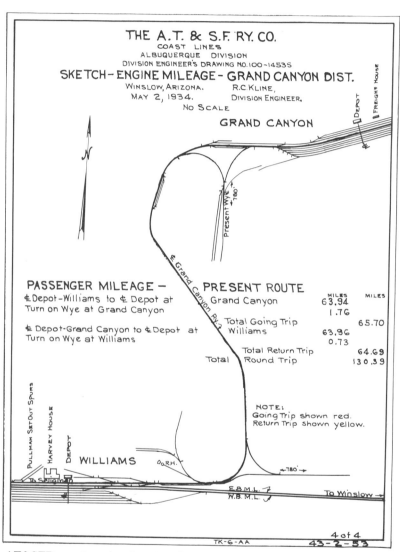

THE A.T. & S.F. RY. CO.

COAST LINES
ALBUQUERQUE DIVISION
DIVISION ENGINEER'S DRAWING NO. 100-14535

SKETCH – ENGINE MILEAGE – GRAND CANYON DIST.

WINSLOW, ARIZONA.   R.C.KLINE,
MAY 2, 1934.   DIVISION ENGINEER.
NO SCALE

GRAND CANYON

PASSENGER MILEAGE –

₵ Depot-Williams to ₵ Depot at
Turn on Wye at Grand Canyon

₵ Depot-Grand Canyon to ₵ Depot at
Turn on Wye at Williams

PRESENT ROUTE

	MILES	MILES
Grand Canyon	63.94	
	1.76	
Total Going Trip		65.70
Williams	63.96	
	0.73	
Total Return Trip		64.69
Total Round Trip		130.39

NOTE:
Going Trip shown red.
Return Trip shown yellow.

WILLIAMS

To Winslow

4 of 4
TK-6-AA   43-2-53

AT&SFRy engineering drawing showing all tracks between Williams and Grand Canyon in 1934. All yard tracks at both locations are detailed. The roundhouse location in Williams is also shown. The track north of the roundhouse went to the stockyards. Many of these tracks and facilities have been retired.

people of the region, for the most part national news stories pre-empted the front page. Stories of the running of a scheduled train from Williams to the Grand Canyon for the first time appeared on the inside pages of the newspapers. On 6 September, an anarchist assassinated President William McKinley. He did not die until the 14th and stories of the assassination, medical treatment, funeral, governmental succession and speculation on plots and anarchists ran for weeks and pushed the railroad off the front pages. It would have been nice to see some banner headlines about the completion of the railroad.

News in Washington, D.C. had little effect on day-to-day life along the railroad and work continued without interruption. After the ballasting came the consolidation of the line with its support facilities along the right-of-way. Sometime between 1899 and 1905 the two companies completed construction of spurs with section crew housing at Pitt (called MP 6.5 at the time), Valle, Willaha, Anita and Apex. To service the locomotives and station at Anita the Santa Fe built two 24 foot diameter steel water tanks with a 12 car water track 2/10 of a mile further up the grade. Extras spotted tank cars on the water track where crews connected them to pipes which gravity-fed the water to cisterns at the station. Section crews also installed spur tracks at Hopi and Coconino stations and bridge & building crews constructed a section house and bunkhouse at MP 18. Completion of the right-of-way by the Santa Fe ended nearly two years of construction on the main line. To this end the two companies installed and ballasted 270,400 ties with 21,634 52 or 56 pound relay rails and their fastenings on a road bed covering nearly sixty-four miles which crossed over 56 bridges and 61 culverts.

SF&GCRR bridge crews constructed the longest and highest bridge on the line just north of Valle over Spring Valley Wash. The pile and frame trestle is reported to have been over 300 feet long and 50 feet high. Around 1918 the Santa Fe replaced it with a 118 foot masonry bridge under earthen fill. Today, the longest bridge on the line crosses Cataract Creek at MP 4. This 182 foot long pile and frame trestle spans the headwaters of a stream system reaching all the way to the Colorado River. Culverts along the line are constructed of either metal, concrete pipe or timber. One hundred twelve curves and twenty-seven grade crossings between Williams and the Grand Canyon also require attention and maintenance. For such a short line there certainly has been enough to keep the roadmaster, section gangs and bridge and building crews busy.

In 1905 the Santa Fe renovated and upgraded several

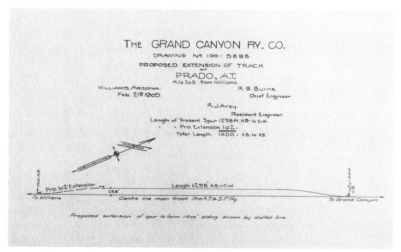

THE GRAND CANYON RY. CO.

DRAWING Nº 100-5898

PROPOSED EXTENSION OF TRACK
AT
PRADO, A.T.
Mile 20.5 from Williams

WILLIAMS, ARIZONA
Feb. 21st 1905.

R. B. Burns.
Chief Engineer

R.J. Aray.

Resident Engineer.
Length of Present Spur 1298 ft. R.B. to End.
" Pro. Extension 102.
Total Length 1400 - R.B. to R.B.

Pro. 102 Extension

258.8'

Length 1298 R.B. to End.

To Williams

Centre line main track The A.T. & S.F. Ry

To Grand Canyon

Proposed extension of spur to form 1400' siding shown by dotted line.

Grand Canyon Railway Company engineering drawing on linen showing the track extension in 1905 at Prado, Arizona Territory.

of the single switch spurs to passing tracks (sidings) with turnouts at both ends. With these improvements longer trains could use the sidings at Red Lake, Prado, Valle, Willaha and Hopi to greater advantage. Facilities along the line began to look more complete. The plan view of the railroad now appeared pretty much in its final form with only a few minor adjustments to be done over the years. Stations along the right-of-way are as follows:

WILLIAMS (MP 0). Southern terminus of the line. Location of a station, wye, telegraph, roundhouse, shops, yards, connection with the east-west mainline, section house and gang and after 1908 a combined Harvey hotel and station. Combined use of the Williams facilities has been in effect by agreements from the time of the Santa Fe & Grand Canyon Railroad and the Santa Fe Pacific Railroad.

PITT (MP 6.5). Location of section house, gang, telephone and a 36 car siding (based on 85 foot Pullman car with allowance for a four unit diesel and heater unit). Originally built as a spur in 1899 the railroad upgraded it to a passing track in 1905. Prior to 1906 company records referred to the section and siding as MP 6.5 and the origin of the name "Pitt," is unknown but it possibly is a corruption of Cinder Pit. Use of the pit commenced in 1906 with the reballasting of the Grand Canyon line and construction of a wye at MP 7 with the spur running east-southeast to the pit. The Santa Fe abandoned use of the pit and retired the spur about 1924. Perrin family descendents, who still own the surrounding land with ownership dating back to the 1880s, do not remember anyone in the region named Pitt for whom

Remains of retired bunkhouse at Valle. The Santa Fe bulldozed these structures to save on tax money.

the siding could have been named. Lilo Perrin expressed emphatically that no cattle or sheep loading operation existed at Pitt as Granger's *Arizona Place Names* states. The Santa Fe retired the siding at Pitt in 1942 and abandoned the section on 1 April 1947.

RED LAKE (MP 9.0). Location of a 31 car siding primarily used for cattle and sheep loading and a telephone. Named for a lake across the highway which takes on reddish hues from Moenkopi silt washed in during rains. The community boasted a post office for a short time in 1888 and a telegraph office operated for a short period in the early 1900s. Originally built as a spur in 1899 crews extended and upgraded it to a siding in 1905 and to its present size in May 1928. Probably abandoned in 1956 with tracks retired in 1974.

BLY (MP 14.9). Location of a nine car spur and a telephone. Built for Fletcher D. Bly by the Santa Fe in April of 1917. The contract included a concrete water tank and corrals for sheep loading. Retired by the railroad on 12 December 1941 material from the spur was used for construction of the spur at MP 18. The crossing at this point is the remains of the Beale Wagon Road.

MP 18 (Actually at MP 18.2). Location of a section house, gang and a telephone. After abolishment of the sections at Valle and Anita in 1941 and 1942, the section at MP 18 became responsible for maintenance of track from MP 10.0 to MP 45.0. The Williams section covered MP 0.0 to MP 10 and the Grand Canyon

45

section covered MP 45 to MP 63.8. The railroad abolished the section on 15 June 1954. At this time and until abandonment of the line the sections at Williams and Grand Canyon split responsibilities for maintenance at MP 39.0. The company installed a 610 foot spur in December of 1941 and in turn, retired it in 1974.

PRADO (MP 20.5). Location of a 23 car siding and a telephone. Originally built in 1899 for cattle and sheep loading by several ranchers. Prado is Spanish for "meadow" and this certainly is a pretty meadow. Renamed Quivero in August of 1908 because there is a larger station named Prado near Corona in California.

QUIVERO (MP 20.5). Supposedly named for Quivera, one of the mythical cities for which Coronado searched in 1540. The reasons for choosing this name or the change of the ending from "a" to "o" are unknown. Originally built as a spur the railroad rebuilt it as a siding in 1905, extended it in 1929 and again in 1931 to its present 23 car siding size. Retirement of siding track and turnouts came in 1974. The Santa Fe built the present loading pens about 1917, rebuilt them in 1936 and in 1974 retired and sold them in place. They are still in use by local cattle and sheep ranches.

VALLE (MP 29.0). Location of a section house, gang, telephone and a 37 car siding for cattle and sheep loading. Originally built as a spur in 1899 the Santa Fe rebuilt it as a siding in 1905 and again extended it in March 1929 to its present size. Named in Spanish for Spring Valley. The railroad built the loading chutes for the Grand Canyon Sheep Company in 1919. It is presently the headquarters of the Bar Heart Ranch which purchased all structures in 1941 when the railroad retired them in place. Cattle are still loaded from this location today but all transportation is handled by truck. This station occasionally appears in the record as ABRA and locals apparently called it Abra Crossing. Abra ceased to be used in the 1930s and it is probably an Anglo corruption of cabra, the Spanish word for sheep. The railroad abolished the section on 19 January 1941 and retired the siding track and turnouts in 1974.

WILLAHA (MP 37.8). Location of a section bunkhouse, telephone and a 24 car siding for cattle, sheep and ore loading. Named after a Supai Indian word meaning "watering place". Originally built as a spur in 1899 the railroad extended and up-graded it to a siding in 1905. The Santa Fe built the watertank, warehouse and corrals for the C. L. DeRyder ranch in 1919 and renovated them in 1940. Leases extended to the Azurite Copper Company in 1903 and the Hougue Mining Company in 1907

Pile and frame bridge over Cataract Creek at MP 4. At 182 feet this is the longest bridge on the Grand Canyon line. The ballast train on the bridge is the first ordered train for the new Grand Canyon Railway. Taken 22 June 1989.

Pile and frame bridge over Coconino Wash at the north end of Coconino station.

provided for copper ore loading. The date of section abolishment is unknown but the Santa Fe retired the siding track and turnouts in 1974.

WOODIN (MP 43.8). Location of a one car spur for cattle and sheep loading. Upgraded to three car capacity on 15 December 1937. Originally built by the Santa Fe in 1917 for the Pittman Valley Land and Cattle Company and later leased to the Grand Canyon Sheep Company in 1930 and again in 1937 to the Babbitt Brothers Trading Company. Unknown as to the origin of the name but a strong possibility exists the Santa Fe named it after W. H. Woodin, president of the American Car and Foundry Company which built railway cars. The railroad retired the siding track and turnout in 1974.

ANITA (MP 44.9). Location of a section house and gang, telephone, stock yards, Forest Service headquarters, school, post office, 40 car wye, 12 car water track, ore loading ramp, the 2.87 mile spur to the Anita Mines (retired in September 1917), a 1,250 foot siding (later shortened in September, 1917 to a four car spur for the Forest Service), two water tanks and a fair sized community. Named for Anita Lombard and originally called Anita Junction when built in 1899. William Lockridge contracted with the Santa Fe for construction of the ore ramp in 1918. On 31 January 1942 the company abolished the section and by 1956 all structures had been removed. All that remains today are the ore ramp and the stock yards, originally built by the Santa Fe in 1909, enlarged in 1913, retired in place, sold in 1974 and still in use by the CO Bar ranch and others. Retirement of track done in 1942 with the exception of the wye which they retired in 1972.

HOPI (MP 50.0). Location of a 23 car siding and a telephone. Most likely installed as a doubling track for the five mile long Anita-Apex grade and later used as a set out for the logging trains from Apex. Named in all probability for the Hopi Indians. Established about 1901 as a spur and later extended in 1905 and again in 1928 the railroad retired the siding on 14 November 1942 with the removal of the rails, switches and switch ties.

APEX (MP 52.0). Location of a section house, gang, telephone and a 31 car siding. Originally built as a passing track in 1901. In 1928 it became the location of the Saginaw and Manistee lumber operations with an 85 car wye and spur. An additional siding held 27 cars. The Santa Fe built these facilities for the Saginaw and Manistee Lumber Company. Apex has been called the high point of the line. Actually the Grand Canyon rim is higher but Apex is at the top of the longest and steepest grade

Remains of the station at Willaha in 1973 showing buildings, corrals and siding. The Santa Fe retired the siding and other facilities in 1974.

James Collection

Remains of Willaha in 1984. Note siding is no longer in place, station sign is missing and buildings have deteriorated.

which is where the name probably originated. On 1 June 1930 the Santa Fe abolished the section and retired the wye and interchange track in 1942 with removal of the rails, switches and ties. The siding remained in service until retired in 1954.

COCONINO (MP 57.2). Location of a 34 car siding built in 1900 as a passing track and a telephone. In 1916 a rancher named Henderson contracted with the railroad for the construction of a concrete box water tank for his cattle. Served temporarily as the northern terminus of the line and transfer point for the Grand Canyon stage while construction by the SF&GCRR and later the AT&SFRy moved north to the rim. Used at least part of the time to set out water cars from the Grand Canyon. Named for the wash in which it is located. Retirement of the siding probably occurred in 1954.

GRAND CANYON (MP 63.8). Northern terminus of the railway with passenger station facilities, telegraph, several tracks used as set outs for trains, a wye for reversing train direction, water tracks for off-loading water into cisterns and tanks and a section gang. Tracks are numbered from 1 to 41 yet the Canyon yards never had 41 tracks at any one time. The Santa Fe relocated, renumbered or combined several tracks over the years. Additionally, tracks bore names related to their function. Track names such as old flume, garbage, oil, gasoline, barn, engine, engine storage, house and power house spur all saw use

Railroad track gang in the early 1900s. Gandy brand tools gave them the name Gandy Dancers. Flaherty Collection, NAU

from time to time. In 1950 engineering drawings placed the car capacity for the yards at 226 with the stem of the wye able to hold a sixteen car passenger train with a four unit freight diesel and heater unit. The section and bunk houses were located along the stem of the wye on the east side. Abolishment of the section occurred on 26 May 1969 and from this time on the Williams section handled any necessary maintenance of the line. The last retirements of tracks came between 13 and 20 June of 1974 with removal of tracks 3, 4, 17, 21, 23, 27, 29, 33, 35 and 37.

On 15 March 1926 the Williams field engineer conducted a survey for a proposed 600 foot spur at MP 48+1686 feet. No reason for this spur is apparent nor is there evidence of it having been built.

At MP 63, within the National Park, the Santa Fe built an ore loading ramp and siding for the Western Gold & Uranium Corporation in June of 1959. This facility serviced the Orphan Mine on the south rim of the Park and the company loaded ore at this location until 23 April 1969. Retirement of the ramp and tracks occurred in 1974 concurrent with the yard retirements.

A telegraph/telephone pole line is located on the right-of-way to the west of the track. An agreement between the Santa Fe and Grand Canyon Railroad and the Postal Telegraph Company on 1 May 1896 gave them access to this line. On the 3rd of December 1899 they made this arrangement a joint venture for the next twenty five years. The Grand Canyon Railway continued this partnership when it took over the line. On 28 December 1920 the Western Union Telegraph Company purchased the Postal Telegraph Company and a new contract effective 1 January 1921 gave Western Union service rights to the Canyon.

Western Union provided telegraph service to the Canyon over these lines from the lobby of the El Tovar Hotel until 1933 when it closed the office and turned over telegraph duties to the Santa Fe operator at the station. When Western Union stopped service the Bell Telephone Company began service along the line and to the canyon.

Signal and communications workers for the Santa Fe maintained the line year-around in all kinds of weather. These important lines provided the primary communications link for the Grand Canyon with the rest of the world. The railroad relied upon them for train orders and section communications. People at the Canyon relied on them for doing their business and general communications. Linemen never considered it unusual to be out in a howling gale or snowstorm looking for a break in the line. Everyone knows lines don't break in nice weather.

51

Track and Bridge & Building gangs rebuilding the roadbed and bridges at Miller Wash after the wreck of 29 July 1916.   Black Collection

For many years the station telegraph operator occupied one of the most respected positions at the Canyon. Without the operator birthday messages and the telegram giving Aunt Martha the arrival time of her favorite niece would not have been possible. In fact, for many years the efficient and safe functioning of the railroads rested in a large measure with the conscientious telegraphers.

Telegraph operators transmitted and received train clearances, work orders, company business messages and Western Union telegrams and money orders. Their responsibilites included the passing of train orders to trainmen by means of bamboo hoops with the order clipped to it. After the engineer or conductor removed the order from the hoop he then dropped it from the train leaving the operator to hike up the right-of-way to retrieve it. Passengers on the trains could also send and receive telegrams by this system.

Over the years telegraphers handled a variety of tasks for the railroad. After the Santa Fe installed the Centralized Traffic Control (CTC) system the telegraphers became part of the main line traffic control. With this system in place their duties expanded to include the throwing of switches and monitoring the blocks in their district. In the event of an accident the dispatcher sent a telegrapher to the site. The operator provided the communication link necessary for safe train movement and transmitted equipment requirements for the crews working to clear wreckage

52

and repair damage.

During the years of World War II, women began to be accepted into the position of telegraph operator. A "brass pounder" held a very responsible and respected position in the railroad. There had never been any reason for it to be otherwise and the position remained male dominated for many years. With the manpower shortages caused by the war the railroads took a considerable step forward and it is much to the credit of their male counterparts these women found themselves readily accepted. Men and women telegraphers worked together on the Santa Fe main and Grand Canyon lines for many productive years. With the advent of teletype machines and improved telephone and radio communications the position of telegrapher faded into the past.

Eventually telephones took over at the Canyon and people along the line began to take advantage of the service. Several ranches erected their own poles from the main line to the ranch headquarters. Some of these lines extended up to seven miles. It might have not been very convenient for people to travel several miles to make a telephone call at one of the stations but that certainly beat driving sixty miles to Williams and back over dirt roads. In medical emergencies alone these lines became worth their weight in gold.

Today the lines are either down or not in service north of MP 40. Some poles have recently been removed for other uses by individuals who do not respect people's property. Newer

Volcanic cinder cone with cinder pit on the lower right slope. Looking northeast from Pitt station at MP 6.5.

lines along the highway service the Grand Canyon. The remaining lines are still in use by ranchers near the right-of-way. These lines are now serviced by the local U S West company.

With the advent of the sections a new way of life came to the region. Section hands, "gandy dancers" if you will, and their families moved into the section houses and bunk houses. Families with school age children usually stayed in Williams while the men worked at the section. Mexican men from Mexico, the Territory and later the State of Arizona filled these positions. In the early 1900s Chinese and Japanese gangs worked along the line but they apparently did not take up residence in the sections along the line. The Japanese lived in carbody dormitories located near the roundhouse in Williams. Chinese laborers usually resided in a district on the southeast side of town. This district at one time held the largest Chinese community in Arizona.

Hard work and long days typified life in the sections along the line. Each section usually had four to six men assigned. When the job required tie replacement every man had a daily quota of fifteen. Men did their own work on ties and didn't help each other unless a new man needed to be taught the tricks of the trade. Tie replacement required a man to pull the spikes, dig out the old tie, pull it out, put a new one in place, spike it to the rail, level it and tamp ballast around the tie for stabilization. Before the days of machinery these men did all of this work with hand tools and each carried his own load and did not depend on others to do his share of the work. As a worker became more experienced he became able to finish faster and he got to take a break until the others caught up with him. The foreman marked ties for replacement when he judged them to be rotted, split or saw that the tie plates had worn the ties excessively.

Initially the railroads used more expensive hardwood ties only on the curves. In later years the Santa Fe changed many others to hardwood also. On this line ties usually have a life span of 20 to 25 years. Normal tie life on heavily traveled main lines is from 5 to 8 years. There are still many ties in serviceable condition on this line with date nails from as early as 1923. In 1984, while walking from the Grand Canyon to Williams along the line, the author found one tie in good condition with a 1904 date nail. Talk about preservation!

Daily work schedules for the sections called for eight hours with the exception of World War II when manpower shortages required ten hour days. Many men left for either wartime service or better paying jobs in the defense plants and this resulted in reduced sections along the Grand Canyon line. Same amount

54

of work with less men equals longer days.

In peace or at war, railroads require maintenance. Ballast needs to be tamped, ties and rails changed as needed and when the Santa Fe overhauled the line and upgraded the rails from 52 and 56 to 65 and again to 85 and 90 and later to 112 pound rail, spikes driven, rail anchors set in place and gauge rods installed to maintain the standard gauge of 4 feet 8-1/2 inches. These men worked hard. Over the seventy-six years this railroad received maintenance everything has been replaced several times. Literally this means several Grand Canyon Railways have been built by these people. Consider that and one begins to get an idea how hard these men worked. Rail is designated in pounds per yard. Therefore, a thirty-nine foot 112 pound rail actually weighs about 1456 pounds. Try to man-handle something like that with track tongs and six people sometime and you will get the picture quite fast.

Shoddy construction by the original builders caused the Santa Fe to completely rebuild the line, including bridges and culverts, in 1907 and 1908. Upgrading of the rail, although done in different sections at different times meant each and every rail, spike and tie plate required replacement a minimum of four times after the original laying of the line. Major overhauls came in 1922, 1924/25, 1927/28, 1930/31 and finally in 1949. Over the years division engineers ordered several realignments to straighten out curves and take advantage of less steep grades.

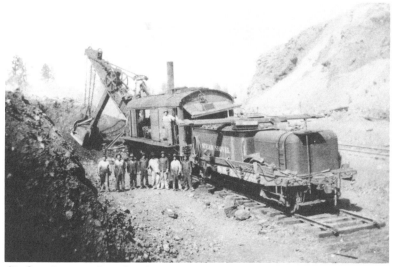

Cinder pit operations in 1914 using oil fired steam shovel on rails. This method is certainly better than loading the ballast into cars with shovels as the Chinese laborers did in 1906-08.   Black Collection

To maintain standard gauge on the more unstable curves of this line the crews installed gauge rods with four or five to the rail being the average. Rail anchors are used sparingly along the line with more in areas near stations and on grades where greater tractive effort is required of the locomotives.

Track work is hard and it can be dangerous. Accident reports over the years give testimony to broken legs and toes from dropped rails. Fingers are frequently mashed by ties shifting and tools slipping. Lacerations caused by flying steel splinters from mauls or spikes are common. Safety is preached as a religion by the Santa Fe but accidents always seem to happen.

Probably the worst accident to befall section workers in the course of their jobs occurred on 29 June 1909. An article in the *Williams News* of 3 July reads,

Explosion At Apex
Three natives of Old Mexico were seriously injured as the result of an explosion of dynamite which occured at Apex fifty-four miles from Williams on the Grand Canyon railroad, Tuesday. One man was so seriously injured that it is expected he will not recover.

The three men were blasting a rock with several other Mexicans belonging to the same section crew and when a discharge of dynamite did not explode within the regulation time the three went back to learn the cause, and explosion followed with a result as above stated.

The railroad transported all of the injured to the Santa Fe hospital at Albuquerque where the one man died of his injuries. Their names never appeared in print.

Construction along the right-of-way required continued use of explosives over the years. To make the line as direct as possible much of it travels up and over or through the very hard Kaibab limestone formation. The only way construction equipment of the day could handle the rock efficiently required it to be blasted into small fragments. Also, the huge Ponderosa pine trees proved to be a barrier to horse teams trying to clear the way. After felling of the trees, crews blasted the stumps loose so they could be moved out of the way. The use of explosives could be deadly as shown above or even provide some spectacular results as seen in this story from 7 September 1901.

A peculiar accident occured near the Bright Angel hotel Wednesday. While the graders were at work clearing

Rowe's Well in 1901 about the time the Grand Canyon Railway reached the south rim. It would expand in later years to include a tourist camp, bowling alley and dance hall.   Museum of Northern Arizona

the right-of-way, a large blast that had been placed under a mammoth stump, shot the stump into the air until it was a mere speck in the sky. It descended into an unoccupied tent near the hotel, completely demolishing it. It then bounded across the street, tearing up another tent. Fortunately, no one was hurt.

For all of the use of explosives on this line over the years these two cases are the only known instances of injury or damage.

Standard Santa Fe 21' X 114' ten room concrete bunk houses provided living quarters for the section crews. The railroad did not provide furniture so if you brought a bunk you slept on a bunk. If not, you slept on the floor. Each room did come equipped with a wood burning stove for heat, however. Running water was available if you had a bucket and ran down to the water barrels or cistern and ran back. The traditional little house away from the house completed the sanitary facilities. Boarding trains also saw use along the line and housed bridge & building crews or supplemental section gangs.

The Santa Fe maintained a store in Williams for their employees and sent food and dry goods by truck out to the sections once a week. They also stocked tools and work clothes. The store only sold the best and most durable qualities. A man wanted his overalls and gloves to take a lot of abuse and last a long time. Railroad personnel made purchases on credit and had the amount deducted from their salary but most of the people did their regular shopping in Williams or at the Grand Canyon as they considered the company store too expensive.

Entertainment was limited to watching jack rabbits or going to a rare social evening and dance at one of the section houses or Williams.

Families, especially those with children, usually lived in Williams. Children attended the Mexican school in Williams or later on the one-room school houses at Anita and Apex if the children lived at the section.

When the Mexican men went in service or left to take high paying jobs in the defense plants during the war the railroad felt the shortage of section hands. At this time the Santa Fe began to hire Indians and in doing so created considerable problems in the field. Supervisors could not speak the language and the Indians had no knowledge of the work required or the safety aspects of the job. It would not be at all unusual for an Indian hard at work to have a train bearing down on him and not be aware of it. The foreman, unable to speak the language, found it difficult to warn crew members of impending danger or to even instruct them in the correct procedures. Also, the Indians were not used to working with schedules and quotas that had to be met and safety rules and regulations. The situation required much changing to be done by both sides in a short time. And change they did. Indians today comprise a large part of the section work force of the Santa Fe and many are foremen.

In these years of completion and rebuilding of the Grand Canyon Railway, one instance of legal difficulty came about in 1906. The railroad needed new ballast. It cost money and time to haul cinders from the cinder pit near Flagstaff. This region is all of a volcanic origin and there are cinder cones all along the line. The cone near MP 6.5 on the Perrin ranch provided the best source of cinders and an easy access.

As usual with the railroads of the time, they considered something they wanted as theirs. This situation proved no exception. They needed ballast and this conveniently located cinder cone had the right size in great quantities. The Santa Fe filed suit in Federal Court in Prescott for condemnation in their favor. Dr. E. B. Perrin is not to be considered a light-weight but the power of the Santa Fe totally out-classed him. The court awarded the cinder cone outright to the railroad.

The Santa Fe wasted no time in building a spur with a wye at MP 7 to the pit. During the original rebuilding and reballasting of 1907/1908, Chinese laborers using shovels loaded cinders in gondola cars. They unloaded the ballast along the line in the same fashion. Up until 1924 this pit provided the ballast for the Grand Canyon line in its several overhauls and day-to-day

Date nails removed from retired ties on the Grand Canyon line. Diamond shaped nails came from bridge beams. ZM nail indicated tie treated with zinc mercuric for preservation.   Blair Collection

needs. Although still owned by the Santa Fe it is no longer in service for the railroad. The State of Arizona leases the pit for its cinder needs on the roads of the area.

During these years the Santa Fe completed all of the major changes along the line. However, much work remained to be accomplished at either end. In August 1901, Williams got its new freight house. A major addition, which restored some of the prominence of Williams as a railroad center, the railroad built a new six stall roundhouse with a turntable. This replaced the eight stall roundhouse moved from Williams to Seligman by the Santa Fe Pacific in 1897. Up until that time Williams had been a division headquarters. As the range and speed of locomotives increased the division moved to Seligman. With the arrival of the Grand Canyon line Williams had again moved out of the railroad backwaters. The motive power for the main line and Grand Canyon Railway jointly utilized these facilities.

Over the years to come the daily work of maintaining what had been so laboriously built became routine. Only minor changes needed to be made in the alignment of tracks and the changeouts as noted above. As demands for manpower increased on the main line they began to decrease on the branch lines such as the Grand Canyon. The Santa Fe reduced sections until finally only those at the Grand Canyon and Williams remained. By the 1950s the railroad bulldozed all of the section buildings with the exception of Apex to save on tax money. Skeletal remains of the bunk house at Apex and rusting trash piles are the only survivors capable of bearing testimony to the living conditions and the way of life at a section along the line.

The railroad retired most of the facilities between the

1950s and the 1970s. Material from spurs and sidings no longer in use had to be reclaimed for use elsewhere. When steam ceased to be the main motive power in 1953 the Santa Fe retired the water towers at Anita. The community of Anita dwindled as the railroad reduced its facilities. The Forest Service changed their headquarters to Tusayan and the families living there relocated to a variety of places. Several of the people moved their houses with them and some can be seen in Williams today.

None of the sidings or passing tracks and few of the trackside structures of what once belonged to The Grand Canyon Railway exist any longer, except in the record of a few surviving engineering drawings and what one can find by walking along the right-of-way. The graded beds are still visible with a few old, rotting ties as reminders of what at one time had been a busy place. Switches are long since gone but the evidence of their position remains. The bulldozed section buildings are merely piles of broken concrete. People once sheltered in these buildings have long ago moved on and the quiet belies the life that once existed here.

During this period of rebuilding two corporate moves occurred to merge the Grand Canyon Railway with the Atchison, Topeka and Santa Fe Railway Company. The first action reduced administrative problems between the "two" companies. The GCRy had no rolling stock or power of its own and had been required to "lease" them and all other equipment from the parent AT&SFRy. Other legal arrangements required by the separation of companies also added to the pile of unnecessary paperwork. The second action alleviated this extra work, by the simple paper expedient of the AT&SF leasing the Grand Canyon Railway. Apparently they did not occupy a position which allowed them to acquire it outright at this time. Possibly some legal or stock problem which could not be resolved proved to be the barrier. A considerable savings in administrative workload must have been achieved by this maneuver as this eliminated the duplication of almost all paperwork involving the "two" companies. With this move came the formal listing of the Grand Canyon District of the Albuquerque Division of the Coast Lines in the timetable of 15 March 1925.

Later, in 1942, The Grand Canyon Railway Company formally ceased to exist. On 31 December of that year, the Records of Incorporation of the State of Arizona show the GCRy being reconveyed to the Atchison, Topeka and Santa Fe Railway Company. Now, with the legal maneuvering complete everything appeared nice and neat. This might have been the case as far as the situation concerned the legal beagles of the AT&SF but everyone still called it the Grand Canyon Railway or the Grand Canyon Line. Traditions die hard.

And the rails of the Grand Canyon Railway are still here as is the name. Hopefully they will be here for a long time to come.

CATTLE & SHEEP

If one is to believe the many range war stories in books and shown on the movie screen, cattlemen and sheepmen have always been at each others throats and always will. Too many of these stories are true and have resulted in some vicious battles but happily this has not been the case with the ranchers in the area of the Grand Canyon Line. Witness to this fact is the funeral of one of the long time cattlemen of the area. Two of his pallbearers were sheepmen. Such a story is not the sensational stuff movies are made of but the facts of life in this region.

Long before the Santa Fe and Grand Canyon Railroad came into being ranchers raised cattle and sheep on the high desert plains of northern Arizona. Ranching and mining comprised the major industries of the region for many years. The railroad surveys of the late 1800s divided the land north and south of the proposed lines into a checkerboard pattern of one mile square sections. Alternate sections were deeded to railroads, individuals or corporations with the remainder belonging to the Territory of Arizona or the United States. The government leased sections out to the owners of adjacent sections for grazing and this remains the practice today.

Prior to 1900 ranchers in the Williams area shipped cattle and sheep from stock yards along the main line of the Atlantic and Pacific Railroad and its successors, the Santa Fe Pacific Railroad and the Atchison, Topeka and Santa Fe Railway. As track moved north from Williams toward the mines at Anita,

Stock extra with 2-10-2 3800 class 3925 in the lead pulls into Williams
after loading sheep at Quivero.   Williams News

Double deck stock car. The Santa Fe used cars of this type along the Grand
Canyon line for sheep and calves.   Flaherty Collection, NAU

the ranchers of the area took advantage of the railroad's presence and began to drive their stock to the closest points along the line for loading. This saved many miles of trail driving to Williams. Until the AT&SF built more permanent yards along the line in the 1910s the ranchers loaded their livestock at roughly constructed pens and chutes. Ranchers contracted with the railroad for construction of these yards along with the necessary spurs, sidings or wyes.

In this manner we see this railroad worked in harmony with the local population. Not only did the railroad build these yards and sidings for the ranchers, it hauled water to them from the wells at Bellemont and Del Rio (later known as Puro) at cost during the dry seasons. Water always has been and remains at a premium in this region during much of the year. The months of April to June and September to November can be counted on to be virtually dry. During these months the railroad became the life line of the cattle and sheep industry in this region and allowed them to operate throughout the year .

The Santa Fe spotted tank cars, usually of 12,500 gallon capacity, at ranches and sidings along the line. A freight extra to the Canyon usually delivered water to the ranches once a week but when needs at the National Park exceeded the supply from Indian Gardens the dispatcher also scheduled water extras. Train and section crews spotted the cars and pinched them into place for dumping into tanks or cisterns. The railroad provided all

Sheep crossing the tracks at Valle. Water tank car is spotted on the siding. View is to the north.   Albers Collection, NAU

of this service for a paltry $18 per car. Even when this cost rose to $28 in the 1960s it continued to be the bargain of the century for the ranchers.

Today, the ranchers are obliged to haul their water from the wells at Williams or Bellemont with their own trucks. Their cost is considerably more than what their "good neighbor" railroad charged. Certainly the railroad did not provide this service merely out of the goodness of its heart. Revenues from cattle and sheep shipments more than balanced the books but hauling stock never really made a lot of money for the railroad. By the 1950s the AT&SF began to extricate itself from the livestock shipping business because the cost of maintaining stock cars started to exceed freight revenues. When the AT&SF cut back on service the ranchers began to move cattle to market by truck. Shipping by truck proved better for the cattle and less costly to the rancher. It also allowed the railroad to slowly and steadily curtail cattle shipments as equipment became unserviceable. During these service reductions the railroad continued to provide water to ranchers along the line at cost.

Cattle and sheep ranchers in this region face several distinct challenges. The water problem is always serious and grass is also at a premium. These problems necessitate the constant moving of the bands of sheep (usually 2,000 to a band) and limiting grazing of cattle to no more than eight or ten head to a section. Due to its austere nature, ranchers consider this to be "60-

Andres Aragon tends his Romney and Rambouallet sheep at Valle in 1938.
Pearson Collection

65

Campero transportation at Valle in 1939. Reliable burros were the preferred pack animals.   Pearson Collection

40 range." Here a cow must have a mouth sixty feet wide and move at forty miles-per-hour in order to find enough to eat.

In the early days stockmen shipped sheep back and forth as the seasons changed along the Santa Fe, Prescott and Phoenix Railway or, as it is usually called, the "Pea Vine" to Wickenberg, Congress and Williams. About 1915 this system became too costly and herders began to trail the herds all over Arizona from east to west and from north to south. Herds in the area of Williams usually numbered about 22,000. At one point in the 1930s about eight million sheep grazed the fields and plains of Arizona. It is difficult to imagine this many sheep on the move.

Tending to these bands of sheep involved quite a variety of people. A caporal had charge of three bands with one herdsman to look after each band while a campero tended to the cooking chores for all of them. Mexican men made up the majority of those who watched over the vast herds of sheep in northern Arizona with a few white cowboys working here and there. In later years Basques came onto the scene and many remain here today. All of them worked hard and long hours with work days being no less than sun-up to sun-down and usually longer.

These herders had well trained dogs working with them except in the spring. This is the time of lambing and the dogs have to be kept away from the ewes. Coyotes then become a major problem. Without the dogs to act as guards the herders have the

Cattle crossing the right-of-way at MP 26. They still present a formidable obstacle to trains.

almost impossible task of protecting the sheep. The coyotes steal into the bands prior to dawn and tear up as many lambs or ewes as they can. It is not unusual for them to kill twenty or more at a time.

Early summer brought the shearing season and with it a time of hard work for all. For many years these men had to shear from forty to fifty sheep per day without the benefit of power tools. This is difficult and tedious back-breaking work. At the end of a day everyone had all they could do to drag themselves to their bed or bedroll.

Wool from the high quality sheep raised in the Grand Canyon district always brought a high demand from the brokers. Wool revenues produced almost as much for the rancher as that realized from the shipping of 50,000 to 60,000 sheep yearly. Until the advent of shipping by truck the ranchers and the railroad had a fairly lucrative relationship.

Sheep ranching is a hard way of life with few opportunities for the more enjoyable pastimes. Those who take up herding sheep usually love the outdoors life on the range. In the days of the vast sheep herds the men always had plenty of food although it tended to be monotonous. Fried mutton, broiled mutton and mutton stew were staples. It was a prized campero indeed who could make mutton taste different from day to day. The herder's dogs and burros usually furnished his only company for days at a time. For the most part entertainment was strictly at the hand of the individual. Shearing time always provided a good excuse for the gathering of friends and family at a barbecue. Everyone came to these events to relax and enjoy themselves as they had finished the back breaking work of shearing. Herders on the trail occasionally found a break from the routine in towns the herds passed by in their continual search for good grazing.

Grazing is the only obvious bone of contention between the sheepmen and the cattlemen of the Grand Canyon district but most have managed to become good friends and remain good friends through the years even with the occasional disagreement over grazing practices. But if asked about the effect of cattle and sheep on the range you will get entirely different answers from the side of the fence you happen to be on.

Cattlemen will tell you sheep trample the grass into oblivion or crop it off at ground level and there are areas that have never reseeded even after many years of nonuse. Sheepmen are quick to point out cattle have over-browsed the protein rich chemiza brush in the area. Even though efforts by responsible ranchers are underway to re-establish this shrub it is a slow process. The high desert does not heal well or quickly. Sheepmen will also tell you cattle will foul the water holes so much so that sheep will not drink from them. Those who raise both cows and sheep don't say much one way or the other. Even in paradise there are differences but these people have found a way to live together in spite of them.

Many of these differences come from abuses of the land. If cattle or sheep are allowed to over-graze then the land will suffer. It all boils down to responsible land use with proper management of the available resources. Smart and responsible ranchers know it is to their benefit to keep the livestock moving from one range to another and allow the land to renew itself. Rotation of cattle to different ranges and the proper animal-to-acre ratio are key tenets of this philosophy. When one takes a look at different ranches it is not difficult to see which rancher takes care of the land and which does not. The cared for ranch boasts a good growth of chemiza and grass while the other has many barren patches and no chemiza. It is easy to blame either the cattle or sheep for over-grazing but in reality the mismanagement of the land by the rancher is the real reason for what has come to be the differences between cattlemen and sheepmen.

Cattle raising in the Grand Canyon region has always been a tenuous business. Water and grass in an arid land are precious, particularly to such large consumers as livestock. On this range no more than ten head to the section can be tolerated

Perrin cowboys herd cattle on the ranch just north of Williams.
Macauley Collection

Perrin cowboys at the Williams stockyards.   Macauley Collection

Loading cattle into stock cars at Williams for transportation to market.
Macauley Collection

even during the best of years. Even so, ranchers raising cattle have a more static situation than that of the sheepmen. Ranch head-quarters usually allow access to most of the ranch with a minimum of difficulty. Before the advent of motor cars and pickup trucks, cowboys were required to spend much time camping out or in line shacks to get the daily work done. On a ranch of 317,000 acres this became a way of life for several men much of the year. Today, with more speedy transportation available, the cowboy can travel further and get more done in a shorter span of time. But many a new pickup truck looks twenty years old its first summer in the field because cowboys will drive it wherever a horse can go. Just because a cowboy has a better means of transportation is not to say the work is any the less hard.

As with his sheepherder counterpart, the range cowboy was left to his own devices much of the year with his supplies being sent out to the various locations. Work was on the sun-up to sun-down schedule. Occasionally the cowboys flagged the Friday night train and headed into Williams for a bit of diversion.

Williams could provide its share of entertainment. In the early 1900s bars, Chinese restaurants and houses of ill repute made up the town's primary businesses. There have always been many respectable people and businesses in Williams but much of the business in the early years came from hard working cowboys,

70

railroaders and loggers. They worked hard and played hard. Some form of action could be found on Railroad Avenue much of the day and night. Fights, knifings and shootings commonly occurred and yet this activity seldom flowed over into the "better" parts of town.

After a Friday night on the town, the cowboys caught their friendly neighborhood railroad back to work on Saturday morning. These hardy souls still had to face a day's work after getting back to the ranch but one wonders just how much work they actually got done after a night in Williams.

The railroad took on the part of a comforting friend and neighbor in this vast country. Ranchers, cowboys and shepherds alike felt a little better and closer to civilization just being able to hear the train or see its lights off in the distance at night. One rancher over by Mount Floyd, which is about thirty miles west of the railroad, used to set his watch by the night train on its way back from the Canyon. It was comforting for all of them to know that if they needed help it really wasn't so far away. A train could be flagged at any time to transport an injured or ill person to the doctor in Williams. The telephones at the various stations along the way also gave them a link to civilization and a means to call for help in times of trouble.

Especially during bad weather and particularly in the winter when roads and trails became impassable the railroad provided a close link with civilization. The unusually severe winters of 1918/1919, 1948/1949 and 1967/1968 hit northern

Babbitt line shack and corral near the retired water siding at Anita. The line shack burned to the ground after this photo was taken. The corral is still in use.

Arizona very hard and the railroad and trainmen were worth their weight in gold to the ranchers during these times.

Exceptionally heavy snow during these years created severe problems and high winds aggravated the situation. Deep drifts foiled any movement and the world all but disappeared when the wind blew the snow into swirling clouds. Ranchers relied on the railroad to keep them in provisions. They called in to Polson's or Babbitt's stores in Williams and placed their orders. Polson or Babbitt people delivered the provisions to the railroad station and the trainmen made the deliveries along the line. These hard winters would have been quite a bit more difficult had it not been for the Grand Canyon Railway and its people.

Even the cattle benefited. During the winter of 1948/ 49, a herd needed to be evacuated from Valle to Williams. The rancher had not expected such a severe winter and planned to winter the herd over. Heavy storms stranded the cattle. Out in the open without food or shelter the cattle would die. A phone call to the ever friendly and helpful dispatchers of the Santa Fe got extras and section hands rolling to Valle in short order. Movement of any kind at the ranch could not be done without the aid of snow cats or bulldozers due to the heavy snow and high winds. Under these conditions a person standing fifty feet away from the tracks at Valle could not even see or hear the train. It took three trains and three days to get the cattle out and down to the shelter of the yards in Williams. In spite of the weather extremes the supreme effort on the part of the railroad, friends and neighbors saved this herd. Thankfully this is the way of these people.

Major cattle and sheep shipments usually occurred in the fall with lambs being shipped in the spring. Stock extras brought the cars to various sidings and spotted them for the ranch hands to load. Ranchers used volcanic cinders for bedding in each car and loaded them as they saw fit. Shipping time usually found twenty to thirty cars spotted at a siding.

After completing the loading the people took time for get-togethers, picnics or barbeques. Shipping points are at locations convenient to several ranches and the occasion provided a good excuse to renew friendships. The wonderful food gave everyone something to talk about for days afterward.

The railroad served the ranchers in many ways and the railroaders were friends. Even under what could be considered less than desirable circumstances they always maintained good relations. However, the prevailing law of the land did bring about a difficult situation with respect to livestock accidents.

Before the railroads arrived in Arizona cattle inter-

The Bar Heart Ranch at Valle station as it appears today. Cattle loading pens are to the right and the ranch headquarters to the left. The crossing is the scene of the accident which took the life of George Barnes.

ests dictated legislation. In that cattlemen were the source of money and power in those days, it is not difficult to understand why the legislature enacted laws to their benefit. With the enactment of the Open Range Law, livestock owners grazed their herds without restriction on the open ranges. In short, cattle and sheep can wander and graze wherever the grass is. If someone does not want the herds on their property then they are responsible for fencing them out. The livestock owner does not have to fence them in.

Fences along rights-of-way are the responsibility of the railroads as provided in the Open Range Law. Under this law any livestock struck by a train are also the responsibility of the railroad. When a train struck and killed livestock, a rancher simply made a claim and the Santa Fe paid fair market value in short order. This was far more than could be expected of other railroads in the west. Most kept ranchers waiting for months to be paid.

Usually the Santa Fe did not want to get in the business of building stock fences. Normally the railroad found it cheaper to pay the ranchers for stock that had been killed than to build fences. Ordinarily this region is not heavily stocked due to the type of range. However, at times some ranchers did bring in large numbers of stock and for whatever reason felt they needed protection.

73

Quivero station as it appeared in 1973. Note telephone booth and scale platform still in place. View is to the south from the siding.

James Collection

Quivero as it appeared in 1984. The siding and telephone booth were removed in the retirement of 1974.

When Lilo Perrin brought in 1200 prime cattle to the area of MP 15-18 in 1948 he considered them worth the expense. Mr. Perrin struck a deal with the Santa Fe to fence both sides of the right-of-way for two and one half miles. Perrin provided the labor for the erection of the fence and the Santa Fe provided the material. This arrangement worked out to the mutual satisfaction of both parties. As long as the Santa Fe didn't have to pay for the labor it became cost effective to protect the 1200 cattle by the purchase of the material. It is almost certain the train crews and the maintenance people who had to clean up the locomotives also appreciated this arrangement.

A few other ranchers along the line also made use of this bargain from time to time. But for the most part, the Grand Canyon line operated under the rules of the Open Range Law without fences. Today's Grand Canyon Railway still operates under these rules.

As we have seen, in many ways railroaders and ranchers came to be family. So it was not out of the ordinary when one of the "rails" gave a puppy to a rancher's young daughter. This puppy grew to be a playful dog whose one great vice in life was to chase Junco birds. Every once in a while the dog would wander a bit far afield when in pursuit of its favorite pastime. On one such occasion it had made its way several miles from home when the crew of the local spotted it. The engineer stopped the train, called the pup in and placed it in the locomotive. Further down the line

Remains of cattle loading chute at Willaha. Red Butte with its remnant Moenkopi formation is in the background.

at the ranch he again stopped the train and the crew hand delivered the dog to its worried owner.

There is no arguing that the Santa Fe built most of the Grand Canyon facilities and literally established the south rim of the National Park as it exists today. Also, there is little to argue that the people at the Canyon had a close relationship over the years with the railroad. But the railroad also built many facilities along the line for the ranchers and supported their businesses. And certainly there is no doubt that the people of the ranches along the Grand Canyon Line had the most personal and close association with the railroad and its people. Like family they shared the good times and the bad. Best of all, they were friends.

Today these people look back and swap stories of the good times and occasionally the hard times come up. In any case, the stories for the most part are good ones. One still hears about the bull elk that moved into the Bar Heart ranch and made himself to home. No one bothered to tell him that he was not a cow so he moved in and out of the herds and corrals just as if this was where he belonged. This went on for a while until the Game and Fish Department decided he needed to be moved. It took a bit of effort to get him under control but they succeeded in loading the elk in a horse trailer and moving him south of Mormon Mountain. Hopefully he found friends as good as he had there at Valle.

All of this came to an end on 1 November 1972, the day of the last rail cattle shipment on the Grand Canyon Line. The Santa Fe spotted eleven cars at Anita and another four at Valle.

The Grand Canyon Railway's southbound number 18 steams through Valle at twilight trailing six Harriman style Pullman cars.   Avery photo

Conductor R. H. Fulton and engineer J. R. Smith hauled this train behind locomotives 3424, 3460, 3352, 3442, 3254, 3411, 3210 and 3390. Twenty two days before on 10 October, the last sheep shipment left out of Quivero in twenty five cars. Conductor J. A. Stanley and engineer M. K. Jennings made this haul with locomotives 3410, 3349, 3239 and 3424. Engine 3424 had the dubious distinction of being a part of both trains which marked the end of an era.

The cattle trucks have taken over entirely what had been the diminishing realm of the Grand Canyon Line. Anyone present with any sense of nostalgia when those trains departed must have felt some remorse as they pulled out for the last time and disappeared over the horizon into history.

The bull elk who came to visit at Valle and decided to stay. No one bothered to tell him he wasn't a cow so he moved right in until the Game and Fish Department came to relocate him.

BUILDING THE GRAND CANYON NATIONAL PARK

With the track of The Grand Canyon Railway reaching the south rim of the Grand Canyon in September 1901, a chapter began with its roots established long before the Santa Fe and Grand Canyon Railroad went into receivership. It is clear in the tone of letters and messages from E. P. Ripley to his subordinates and replies from them, that the Atchison, Topeka and Santa Fe Railway made plans and provisions for construction of facilities at the south rim as early as 1899. When letters from Buckey O'Neill to Ripley and Chairman Aldice on the subject of tourism are considered it becomes a certainty. Apparently the situation involved a waiting game. Waiting for the inevitable financial collapse of the SF&GCRR. Waiting, with a few subtle helpful shoves, for what became a wholly owned AT&SFRy operation.

In 1901 the Grand Canyon National Park did not exist. The federal government offered limited protection to the region under the auspices of the Grand Canyon Forest Reserve. When Theodore Roosevelt first visited the area in 1903, the Canyon, with all of its magnificent natural beauty, so impressed TR he became determined to set it aside as a public trust. Even with his help Congressional action, or inaction, took until 1908 to establish part of the Canyon as a National Monument under the Forest Service. Congress finally established the National Park Service as part of the Interior Department in 1916 and in 1919 the Grand Canyon finally reached National Park status. Between the time the Santa Fe reached the rim and the establishment of the

Aerial view of Grand Canyon Village taken about 1935. Part of the yards are visible along with the new power house, Kolb and Lookout Studios, Bright Angel Hotel (before renovation-note the tent cabins) and El Tovar.

National Park Service

Park, it became the driving force that opened up and developed this spectacular place for all to see. For this, and for doing it in a manner that did not detract from the natural wonder itself, the American people owe the Santa Fe a considerable debt of gratitude.

There are those who would disagree with the above statements and believe the park should have been left completely natural with no signs of human habitation. A nice thought, but hardly realistic. Even today, the Canyon remains off the beaten track and the Santa Fe became the transporter and the provider for those who visited the south rim over these many years. Had it not been for the railroad many millions of people might never have had the pleasure of seeing this wonder and the Canyon is as much theirs to see and visit as those who prefer a more primitive scene.

Consider also that the railroad planners showed restraint and good taste in developing the park without defiling the natural surroundings with one possible exception, the smokestack on the powerhouse. In 1901 the railroad arrived upon a scene bordering on chaos. Tent camps and nondescript hotels cluttered the rim in the vicinity of the Bright Angel trail with no plan or thought of esthetics. Over the years the Santa Fe organized or replaced these camps with the structures that now grace the south rim. With the engineering skills and technology of the times the AT&SFRy made a wonderful contribution which has allowed

The Cameron Hotel about 1903 with the original Kolb studio in the foreground.   National Park Service

generations of Americans and people of the world to experience this great place without insulting their sensibilities.

Naturalist John Muir could not find it in himself to complain of the trains and development at the south rim. When he visited the Canyon late in 1902 he had occasion to write,

> ...when I saw those trains crawling along through the pines of the Cocanini [sic] Forest and close up to the brink of the chasm at Bright Angel, I was glad to discover that in the presence of such stupendous scenery that they were nothing. The locomotives and trains are mere beetles and caterpillars, and the noise they make is as little disturbing as the hooting of an owl in the lonely woods.

In truth, most of the railroad lies in a depression behind the rim with the exception of one short space at the Bright Angel fault and overlook. Most of the natural stone and wood buildings are behind the rim and to even notice them one is required to look away from the overpowering beauty and vastness of the Canyon. Even when viewed from the air or Maricopa Point the community blends quite well into the rolling terrain of the forests. Why complain about something as small as the Grand Canyon Village and the railroad when one is surrounded by a natural phenomenon so vast no one will ever see or understand it

Train coming into the original Grand Canyon station about 1905. The locomotive is possibly 282 on one of its last runs. NAU Special Collections

all?

A common question arriving passengers asked at the station points up how well this community blended into the surroundings. "How do you get to the Grand Canyon?" Newly arrived dudes probably drove the station personnel to drink with the frequency of this question and today, with the advent of the rejuvenated Grand Canyon Railway, people still ask.

As early as 1892 both crude and elaborate tourist accommodations occupied the more choice and accessible locations along the rim. Bright Angel camp handled the hardy few who made their way to the Canyon by way of stage coach or wagon. This tent camp of canvas covered, wooden framed "cabins" furnished with cots or beds of dubious comfort provided for the guests. Cooks produced meals in a dirt-floored tent, which functioned as a kitchen, and then served them in another wooden-floored "dining room." Much of the provisions and bedrolls for these guests arrived with them in either a wagon additional to the coach or as a trailing wagon behind the coach. Not first class but certainly adequate. As rustic as these facilities might have been, the travelers probably considered them a welcome sight after the rugged journey of from ten to eighteen hours.

By the mid 1880s several stage and livery companies operated out of Flagstaff, Williams and Ash Fork. Some provided only transportation to the available facilities on the south rim and others ran to cabins and hotels they themselves established for the tourist trade. Fernando Nellis operated out of Williams to facilities at Grandview Point owned by John "Cap" Hance and William Hull. This log cabin structure did not offer much in the way of creature comforts but it offered a panoramic view of the Canyon and access to the caverns below the Point with their crystal and stalactite formations. Hance and Hull also started the first stage service to the Canyon from Flagstaff.

W. W. "Billy" Bass and Martin Buggeln also ran liveries and coaches and operated tourist accommodations at the rim in addition to transporting passengers from communities south of the Canyon. Bass ran from Williams and later from Ash Fork to the west rim (so-called because it is west of the south rim or Grand Canyon Village area at Bright Angel). Here, for many years, he operated Bass Camp and later Bass Hotel. His camp offered rough living and visitors to the small, wooden hotel did not fare much better but Bass Camp had as its drawing card the magnificent tributary canyon to the Grand Canyon of the Colorado River called Supai Canyon, Havasu Canyon or Cataract Canyon. This is the beautiful home of the Havasupai Indians with its lush

The Bright Angel Hotel with Buckey O'Neill's cabin to the right on the south rim of the Grand Canyon.   Creavy Collection

Tent kitchen for the original Bright Angel Camp about 1900. Note the fresh cooked pies on the table.   Creavy Collection

valley, blue waters, travertine pools and spectacular water falls. It is difficult to get to but Bass had the exclusive on this route.

Bass later worked out an arrangement with the AT&SFRy for a flag stop at MP 59. Here passengers detrained and traveled to Bass Camp via coach. They made the return trip by simply flagging the train at the same location.

Buggeln worked out of Williams with Grandview Point as his destination. Here he built a comfortable, reasonably modern two story hotel. As the largest hotel on the rim around the turn-of-the-century, the Grandview provided the finest lodgings at the Canyon. With Buggeln's and Hance's hotels providing some of the better service at the rim most tourists considered Grandview to be the best accommodations available.

Grandview even held the distinction of being the first post office at the rim under the name of Tourist with Hance as the postmaster from May 1897 to April 1899. What happened to this post office between 1899 and March 1902 is not clear. When the railroad came to the rim in 1901 Buggeln went to work for the Santa Fe at Grand Canyon and he accepted the position of post-master there in March 1902. Interestingly enough, the post office at Grandview was reestablished in November 1903. This time with the name Grandview and Harry Smith as postmaster. Again short lived, it lasted only to November 1908. Both the Hance's and Buggeln's hotels have since been destroyed by the Park Service in order to restore the area to a "more natural site."

Several other enterprising individuals built facilities

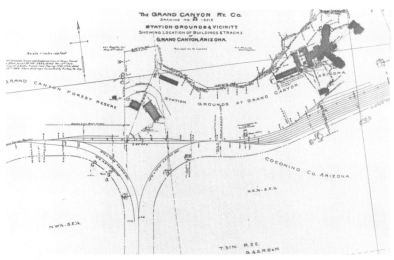

1905 Grand Canyon Railway Company engineering drawing showing the wye and the new El Tovar Hotel. Santa Fe Railway

in the vicinity of the present Grand Canyon Village in the 1890s. Buckey O'Neill built a cabin and bunk house, Sanford Rowe established Rowe's Well and the Cameron brothers erected the Grand View Hotel.

Buckey O'Neill built his log cabin and bunkhouse late in 1896 on the rim where the present day Bright Angel Lodge is now located. It is possibly the first built and is certainly the oldest surviving structure at the Grand Canyon Village. The cabin is still part of the Bright Angel complex. Buckey probably built the small cabin for his own use and the entertainment of friends while at the rim. He eventually divided it into two rooms and later sold it to Ralph Cameron prior to leaving for his date with destiny in Cuba.

Sanford Rowe bought out the Williams livery business of Billy Bass in 1892 and spent the next several years supplying the south rim business people with their freight requirements. He staked some mineral claims about three miles west and south of the village and built a small log hotel there. Over the years it grew into a tourist complex with a hotel, cabins and an entertainment facility which included a bowling alley. A popular spot with the residents of the village the "watering hole" provided some relief from the ever present tourists. Here, they could get away and have a friendly drink, bowl a few lines and do some dancing. By the late 1950s many of the wooden frame and log buildings had deteriorated to a condition beyond repair and demolition by the Park

The El Tovar Hotel and depot shown with the first Grand Canyon Railway train from Williams to the Grand Canyon on 11 September 1989.

85

Service became necessary to ensure safety and the esthetics of the natural scene. In April of 1961 the Park removed the last structures and all that remains today of Rowe's Well is a picnic ramada next to the tracks.

The Cameron brothers, Niles and Ralph, were up to their ears in their mining interests and the Bright Angel Trail. These mines never did produce an ore sufficiently rich to be worth production but the claims gave them a good excuse to exercise their right to the trail and charge a toll of one dollar per animal for its use. They spent many years in hassles with the Santa Fe and Harvey Company over these rights. During the course of these battles Ralph Cameron became a Territorial Representative and later a United States Senator which helped them get legislation passed giving control of the trail to Coconino County. In turn, the Camerons received authorization from the County to continue collecting tolls. Prior to this the Camerons built the Grand View Hotel completing it in 1897.

J. W. Thurber, possibly in partnership with Cap Hance, began to build the Bright Angel Hotel in 1896 and finally finished it in 1900. It started out as a building previously built at another location which he moved to the site and later added a second floor. It became the center for the hodge-podge Bright Angel Camp. Sold about 1902 to the Santa Fe, Martin Buggeln managed it until 1905. It remained in place until 1935 and then the railroad demolished it to make way for the Bright Angel Lodge.

Several other people came to the Canyon during this time to establish tourist related businesses. Beginning in 1889, John Verkamp sold general merchandise and tourist items from a tent. As with the tourist accommodations that came before him this established method with its low overhead served him well and his business prospered for seven years. In 1905 he began construction of the present day Verkamp's Souvenir store. The 18 March 1905 issue of the *Williams News* noted, "The United States has granted to John G. Verkamp, of Flagstaff, the right to one acre of land near the big hotel [El Tovar] at Grand Canyon, with the right to construct a building for a 'curio' business. It is rumored that Mr. Verkamp will begin at once to construct an elegant building on said land." John Verkamp opened his doors on 31 January 1906 and his store and business still remains in the family. Little changed over the years; the building went through a major facelift in 1989 and still anchors the east end of the historic district.

A Grand Canyon legend who established another notable business arrived after the railroad. Emery and Ellsworth Kolb moved their photography shop from Williams to the Canyon in 1903. An account of their exploits on the Colorado River and within the Canyon are far beyond the scope of this record. However, their presence had a considerable effect on some of the buildings on the rim as they had a running squabble with the Santa Fe and Fred Harvey companies who wanted their business for themselves and with some individuals in the Park Service who just wanted them out. The Santa Fe built the Lookout Studio behind the Bright Angel Lodge on the rim at the request of the Harvey Company in an attempt to keep business away from the Kolb studio. This turned out to be one occasion where the powerful railroad and Harvey companies were not to have their way.

The Kolbs, in an agreement with Ralph Cameron, had built their tent studio on the edge of the rim just to the west of the Bright Angel Hotel and overlooking the head of the Bright Angel trail. They relocated in 1904 to the toll house the Camerons had built. This location gave them a guaranteed lock on photographs of tourists going down the trail on the Cameron mules and later on the Harvey mules. Harvey management saw a loss of revenue and did everything in their power from political maneuvering to outright slander in an effort to dislodge the Kolbs.

The Harvey Company took on a worthy opponent. The Kolbs built their original studio in 1904 and added to it in 1915 and 1925. When Emery Kolb died in 1976 at the age of 95 he and the building were still there. His studio and home is now vacant

Shriner specials on 28 March 1937 with 1300, 3500 and 3700 class double headed locomotives providing the power.   National Park Service

and owned by the National Park Service but is scheduled for renovation and reactivation. This historic structure will be a part of the Canyon scene for many years to come.

The Babbitt Brothers Trading Company with their general merchandise store arrived on the scene in 1905. This operation also opened in a tent and in 1921 the Santa Fe built for them the store across the tracks from the present station many people yet remember. Success in business has been their forte and this venture proved to be no exception. They are still doing business at the Canyon in a modern supermarket.

From the time of their arrival in September 1901 as The Grand Canyon Railway, the Atchison, Topeka and Santa Fe Railway Company began to carry out their plans and construction, or at least maintenance and rebuilding, never seemed to stop. Although the GCRy operated legally as a separate company, with the power to make its own contracts, hire and fire, and publish their own timetables, it remained in fact a part of the AT&SFRy. It is not at all unusual to find engineering drawings of structures at the Canyon having one or the other company listed in the legend. No matter, the money and resources all came from the same place.

The parent AT&SF brought to bear much of its facilities, engineering staff and equipment on this project. With some notable exceptions, the Santa Fe bridge & building crews built and maintained the vast majority of the structures at the Canyon. They first built the board and batten station to the north of the main line tracks across from the legs of the wye. The railroad had a twenty acre station grant and they needed every bit of it for the planned station and yards. Eventually they constructed and maintained over six hundred structures at the south rim.

In 1904 Santa Fe introduced the Fred Harvey Company to the Grand Canyon. Since the 1870s Harvey had been running the depot hotels and restaurants for the Santa Fe on a verbal agreement sealed with a handshake. Lawyers of both companies, not conversant with the honor involved in the handshake agreement, finally got their way and formalized this arrangement in 1891 after a short court battle. It resulted in a written agreement which called for the Fred Harvey Company to provide dining car service on all of the Santa Fe trains.

The Harvey Company came to the Canyon in full storm. They, along with the Board of Directors of the AT&SF, determined to make the first major project, the El Tovar Hotel, a showplace. Santa Fe management wanted to clean up and organize the Village in a manner in accordance with their own plan

Rose Bowl special coaches and Pullmans jam the yards at the Grand Canyon.   National Park Service

which included the elimination of all competition. As they found out, this did not entirely turn out to be the way of things.

El Tovar should have been named after a lieutenant of Francisco Coronado's expedition who, in 1540, became the first non-Indian to see the Grand Canyon. But Don Garcia Lopez de Cardenas already had the honor accorded to him of having the hotel in Trinidad, Colorado named after him. So, they named the hotel after his superior who had never seen the Canyon. Don Pedro de Tovar would have been proud of the magnificent structure bearing his name.

Up to this time, the Santa Fe built its depots and Harvey Houses of functional stone, brick or board and batten style construction. The El Tovar became the first major departure from these styles. Proudly described in the Santa Fe brochure after opening in 1905, the El Tovar was then, and is now today a beautiful building resting on the rim of the Canyon.

El Tovar is a long, low, rambling edifice, built of native boulders and pine logs from far-off Oregon. The width north and south is three hundred and twenty-seven feet and from east to west two hundred and eighteen feet. ... The hotel is from three to four stories high. It contains more than a hundred bedrooms. ... Ample accommodations are provided for 250 guests. ...Out-side are wide porches and roof gardens. ... El Tovar is more than a hotel; it is a village devoted to the

89

entertainment of travelers.

Not bad for the wilds of the Arizona Territory.

Building this flagship hotel of the Grand Canyon must have been a considerable strain on the contractor. For the most part, supplies came from Williams. The Polson Brothers store had a standing order with the contractor for materials to be delivered weekly on site at the Canyon by the railroad. One item never changed during the course of construction. A case of "good scotch" apparently helped to fortify the contractor for his daily trials and tribulations. As the Polsons did not stock liquor, a clerk purchased the whiskey weekly from one of the local saloons and put it on the train with the rest of the order. One might wonder how the contractor billed the Santa Fe for these "essential materials."

These Canyon facilities needed electric power and steam for light and heat. To provide this service the railroad constructed a boiler house and pumping plant next to the tracks and south of El Tovar. Originally built in 1905 and enlarged in 1911 and again in 1913 as the Village grew, it lasted until 1926 when the Santa Fe erected the new power plant. By 1924 the National Park Service devised a master plan for the Grand Canyon Village. It required a new power house to meet the demands of the rapidly expanding park and they recommended to the AT&SF that one be built as soon as possible. Wasting no time the railroad engineers began the planning and building almost immediately

Specials filling the yards emphasize the last two curves on the Grand Canyon line. El Tovar is on the left.   National Park Service

90

after receiving the temporary permits to do so.

The Santa Fe laid water and steam lines to the buildings throughout the Village even before the construction of the power house began. Concrete and steel construction with a natural limestone exterior formed the major structure. Limestone from the tail of the wye and from other locations within the park made this relatively large building blend in as much as possible with the local setting.

Only one part of this complex did not fit in—the over two hundred foot smokestack. This sore thumb defiled the natural scene until the plant closed in 1956 and the smokestack was torn down—for the second, and last, time.

During construction of the stack in 1926, Santa Fe engineers realized it was out of plumb and a hazard, so far out of plumb it could be seen just by looking at it. They tore it down and started over. Although it looked ugly, smoke from the steam boilers and the huge diesel motors for the generators needed to be lifted above the community in order for it to be carried away by the wind. Power today comes from hydroelectric sources above the Canyon on the Colorado River near Page. Now used as a storage facility by Harvey, the powerhouse is still in use. But thankfully the smokestack no longer violates esthetics.

Oddly enough, the power plant with its ugly stack never produced pollution at levels which visually obscured the Canyon. The coal fired plant at Page is presently under attack for the pollution levels it has introduced into the Canyon. Built without scrubbers, it is a constant source of smoke and haze in the Canyon.

There are those who do not miss the power plant being in operation because of the stack and the smoke, but the plant provided some lighter moments. Every day at eight AM, noon, one and five PM, the whistle blew to signal the work day start, lunch and quitting time. Dudes startled by the whistle, asked, "What's that?" "Oh that's just the steamboat pulling in to the dock on the river," the locals replied. With that, the dudes headed for the rim to see the steamboat. How many of them "saw" the steamboat is not known, but it is certain that some surely did.

During the early years at Grand Canyon, a doctor attended to the medical needs of residents and tourists in a carbody office located at the end of track on the south side of the yards. At this minimal facility the doctor hardly did more than give physical examinations, treat minor illnesses and provide emergency treatment prior to sending the patient on to Williams or Flagstaff. When the Santa Fe built the hospital in 1929 the level of medical care available improved considerably but doctors continued to use the carbody for office visits well into the 1930s.

In 1902 the Harvey Company made a decision which had far reaching effects on the face of the Grand Canyon Village and other tourist facilities at the Canyon. They hired Mary Elizabeth Jane Colter as an architect and interior designer. She stamped an indelible imprint on the image of the Santa Fe and Harvey companies with her version of a natural style of Pueblo Indian architecture. The Grand Canyon will bear fine evidence of her work for many years to come.

El Tovar received her distinctive touch when she came on the scene in 1905. Doing the cocktail lounge in her trademark style, she apparently experimented and practiced before she began work on her first major structure at the Canyon, the Hopi House. Colter made use of the Hopi culture and designed it to look like a pueblo. At the direction of the Harvey Company, the Santa Fe built it between the El Tovar and Verkamp's Souvenir Store to provide direct competition with Verkamp's. Completed in 1905 it served for many years as the focal point of Indian dances put on by Porter Tomichi and his Hopi family. These dances provided an important part of Santa Fe and Fred Harvey advertising. To this end the railroad constructed an Indian Dance Platform in October of 1951.

Her next efforts came in 1914 when she designed and built the Lookout Studio and Hermit's Rest. As previously noted, the Santa Fe constructed Lookout Studio by Harvey Company request to provide direct competition to the Kolb Studio. Colter surely did not have this in mind when she designed a roughly contoured building that almost blended in with the edge of the rim. It is an example of the art that a fine architect can produce. She also did Hermit's Rest in the same unobtrusive manner. Built at the end of the west rim drive it fit in to the rim almost as if it came to be there naturally. These may well be two of her finest works.

Phantom Ranch, in the bottom of the Canyon on Bright Angel Creek where it meets the Colorado River, received her attentions in 1922. She designed these accommodations as a rustic ranch for the use of the mule passengers and hikers of the Bright Angel and Kaibab Trails. In 1934 a swimming pool built next to the creek and fed its waters offered a refreshing swim. Over the years Phantom Ranch has been updated and is still in use today and well worth the trip. Although the inner canyon is a place of beauty it can be a harsh and changing environment. Probably due to its rustic and sturdy construction, Phantom Ranch withstood the power of a major flood on Bright Angel Creek in 1966.

1902 combination mail and baggage car of a type that serviced the Canyon.   Flaherty Collection, NAU

Sadly enough, the swimming pool did not survive the flood and it has not been rebuilt.

The Desert View Watchtower, probably Colter's most famous work at the Canyon, stands at the easternmost limit of the Park. Perched on the rim and overlooking the eastern stretches of the Canyon and the junction of the Little Colorado River with its big sister, the tower provides a fantastic view to all points of the compass. Arizona's highest mountains, the San Francisco Peaks can be seen from the tower to the south. Over 12,000 feet high and seventy miles away they appear to be but a short distance on a clear day. No further away are the multi-colored formations of the Painted Desert. Stretching across the horizon these ribbons of color make the short climb to the top of the tower worth every step. Here too, for many years, the Hopi put on snake dances to entertain the tourists.

In 1935 the Bright Angel Hotel showed its age and it was something less than a quality facility when Colter turned her talents to its renovation. She totally changed the concept, demolished the old hotel and slowly the new lodge began to take shape. Several of the original structures on the site had a rustic charm and Colter showed her appreciation for things historic. Instead of destroying them she made use of existing log buildings such as O'Neill's cabin and the original Grand Canyon post office and incorporated them into the overall plan. Logs and wood became her primary medium instead of natural rock. The hand squared logs of the old cabins probably provided her inspiration. A geological fireplace with representative natural stone from every horizon in the Canyon formed her signature masterpiece. The separate cabins, including the old post office, offer more private accommodations for the tourist and are reminiscent of the old tent camp. Bright Angel Lodge looked new but it already possessed a history.

Her next and last projects at the Canyon came in 1936 and 1937. The Men's Dormitory and the Women's Dormitory helped to alleviate the chronic housing shortage for Harvey employees at the south rim. Employees who work primarily in the hotel service trades reside at these dorms. The Harvey Company held considerable respect for Colter's work at the Canyon. Therefore they considered it quite fitting to name the women's dormitory in her honor and Colter Hall still bears her name today. Although Mary Jane Colter's work came to a close at the Canyon with these projects the work of the AT&SF and Fred Harvey companies continued.

Ralph Cameron still charged his one dollar per animal on the Bright Angel Trail but Harvey ran tours along the rim in horse drawn carriages and sent mule trips down the Hermit Trail. The Santa Fe completed horse and mule barns along with a blacksmith shop to service these animals in 1907. In these early years Martin Buggeln ran the livery business for the AT&SF and Harvey. His prior expertise in this field made him a natural for the position.

Hotels, camps and dining facilities have always been important considerations for tourists at the south rim. Certainly

Rose Bowl specials at the Canyon on 4 January 1936 with double headed 1300 and 3800 class locomotives in the lead.   National Park Service

the scenery is the reason for coming to the Canyon but everyone needs a place to stay and eat. However, one area of concern at the south rim for tourists and residents alike always will take precedence over any and all others.

Water remains one of the most vital concerns for the Grand Canyon National Park. Initially, the railroad hauled water from Williams in tank cars. Every train literally carried its own supply. After they built cisterns, water specials made the trip to the Canyon on demand with fewer cars in the winter and more in the summer when the most tourists were present. Old photographs almost always include water cars in the background on a siding. A water delivery track, number 4, at the west end of the yards serviced the hotels. Later the Santa Fe moved water operations to the south side of the yard opposite the new station. Track 21 had a flume along side which gravity fed water from the cars to storage tanks from 1911 to 1925. Later, they built a water delivery track to the east of the stem of the wye and designated it track 35. Pipes, with hose connections for fourteen cars, transferred the water to steel storage tanks directly from the cars.

All of this water came from either Flagstaff, Bellemont or the primary source, Del Rio. Del Rio (later changed to Puro), is a station on the "Pea Vine," the Ash Fork to Phoenix run. Spanish for "from the river" Del Rio is located in one of the few valleys in northern Arizona with a year-around supply of water.

The Freedom Train visits the Grand Canyon on 16 February 1949.
National Park Service

Summer supplemental water train on 7 August 1961 dumps 204,000 gallons from Puro.   National Park Service

This source is 122 rail miles from the Canyon and the Santa Fe used it until the last deliveries made in the sixties. The AT&SF hauled water to the Park for the use of the railroad customers and the residents just as it did for the ranchers, at cost. Few, if any, railroads have been so willing to provide a service to its customers on this scale (up to a high of 250,000 gallons per train load). Of course, no water, no customers but the Santa Fe could have charged enough to make a profit and did not.

Water conservation has always been a primary concern of the inhabitants of the Canyon and the railroad. To this end the engineering staff of the AT&SF designed and built a water reclamation plant in 1926. Hailed as a major engineering achievement, it drew visitors from around the world who also needed water reclamation projects. The railroad later expanded the plant's capacity in 1934 to meet the needs of the soon to be completed Bright Angel Lodge and it is still in operation today.

Never designed to provide drinking water, it merely took waste water and turned it into a usable water for the locomotives, vegetation and the sanitary facilities of the Village. Good sense dictated good drinking water should not be used for these purposes. A small problem arose in the delivery of this reclaimed water to the proper facilities without mixing it with the drinking water. Not too many places in this world have pink and blue water pipes but the Grand Canyon Village does. Water for drinking and general human consumption is delivered by the blue

The Fray Marcos Hotel and Williams train station about 1927. People generally referred to this as the Williams Harvey House.

Baumgartner-Leonard Collection

pipes. Delivery to the locomotives, vegetation and the sanitary conveniences is made by the pink pipes. In this way it is a simple matter for the maintenance people to identify the proper line and to not mix the two water sources.

As admirable as this engineering achievement is, it did not solve the water problems at the Canyon. Indian Gardens, below the rim on the Bright Angel Trail, usually has a reliable supply of water. The problem of how to get the water two thousand feet up to the rim required some new technology and again, the Santa Fe engineering department went to work. In 1931 they built a pump house and a pipe line from Indian Gardens to the south rim. Before they could begin the construction of the pump house a cable tramway to haul equipment and materials to the site needed to be built. The water line required a total of two and one half miles of pipe installed from the pump house up the wall of the south rim. After completion of the project they removed the tram.

When the Santa Fe completed this engineering marvel and put it in operation in 1932, Grand Canyon Village had a good supply of water. The Indian Gardens pipeline eliminated the need for a regular water train. However, when required maintenance of the system shut it down or when people used more water than the system could provide, the dispatcher scheduled water extras from Puro. Railroad water supply on an "as needed" basis continued until 1968 when the Park Service got its trans-canyon pipeline from Roaring Springs into regular operation. Even with these supply systems water conservation and reuse at the Canyon will remain a high priority.

With operations at the south rim well under way in 1907, the AT&SF began another project at the south end of the line in Williams. Construction started on a much needed Harvey House, restaurant and depot. The original Harvey facility of several box cars with lunch counters south of the tracks across from the station left a lot to be desired. The Fray Marcos Hotel replaced this with a first class establishment. All appeared as spit and polish on the interior with the usual Harvey southwestern trappings but the exterior did not reflect the style of what had become "traditional" for these two companies. The design of the exterior defies precise classification. Depending on which architect describes the structure one might find it referred to as Greek revival, classic revival or Beaux Arts classic. Whatever the correct terminology, the Fray Marcos is not the traditional Harvey style.

Beginning with design in 1905 and construction in 1907, the Santa Fe completed and opened the Fray Marcos for service on 10 March 1908. Designed by architect Francis W. Wilson of Santa Barbara for the Santa Fe Railway, it is the earliest known use of and the oldest existing reinforced, poured concrete building in Arizona. The Fred Harvey Company managed the hotel and restaurant.

An interesting note about the original design is reflected in its flat, poured concrete roof. Obviously Wilson was not knowlegeable about northern Arizona winters and the snow-loads that can be generated in some of the storms. It did not take long for the roof to leak like a sieve when the accumulated snows melted

Lobby of the Fray Marcos Hotel in Williams about 1927.
Baumgartner-Leonard Collection

and worked their way through the obliging concrete. Instead of spending the money for wooden or metal framing to peak the roof and drain off the water, the Santa Fe hoisted tons of readily available volcanic cinders to the roof, formed them into peaks and added a covering of asphalt roofing. Oddly enough, for as long as they maintained the asphalt roofing it remained intact. As the building became derelict in later years, water poured down through the structure and caused considerable damage which proved very costly in renovation.

When the doors opened for business the hotel and restaurant provided train passengers, tourists and Williams residents with the high quality service and meals for which the Harvey Company is known. It also became the centerpiece of Williams social life. Harvey Girls served meals at either lunch counters or dining room tables. A curio shop provided Indian goods and other items for sale.

The original design had accommodations for guests in twenty-two rooms and another ten for staff, all on the second floor. Room 5 is a two room suite with its own bath and overlooks the tracks. Rooms 7 & 8 and 13 & 14 have a shared bath. Guests in all other rooms utilized a community bath and toilet. The Santa Fe made several changes and additions to the original building over the years and the first, as early as 1909, up-graded utilities and facilities and cost $35,000. Company carpenters and masons handled all additions and renovations. A two story addition in 1925 gave the hotel an additional twenty-one rooms. Built in adjoining pairs, twenty of the rooms have a private bath. They

Seated dining area of the Williams Harvey House which was separated by a wall from the lunch counter.   Baumgartner-Leonard Collection

included one two room suite with a fireplace on the northwest corner of the addition as an apartment for the hotel manager.

The Fray Marcos served for many years to anchor the southern end of the Grand Canyon line. Retired by the Santa Fe in 1954, the hotel remained dormant while the station continued to service east-west main line and Williams-Grand Canyon train traffic. Although technically retired, parts of the hotel did see usage by crews building the Johnson Canyon by-pass in 1960-61. The Williams Elks Club leased it from 1 March 1963 to 1 April 1983. Their contract gave them use of the kitchen, dining area, lobby and curio room. Santa Fe maintenence crews and the field engineer used the station facility until 1988.

Rehabilitation by the Grand Canyon Railway company began 29 March 1989. Initial plans call for use of the station and portions of the Fray Marcos as a passenger facility for its steam trains to the Grand Canyon and for a museum dedicated to the historical preservation of the railroad and the cultural history of the region. Future plans call for the second floor to be renovated as company offices. Time, with its inevitable changes, has taken so many of the wonderful old Harvey Houses from us. At least we are not losing this one.

With most of the building at the Canyon and Williams completed, the AT&SF and Harvey companies settled down to mostly routine maintenance with repairs and painting as needed. Railroad paint and repair crews took care of most of this work. Section gangs handled the yard work of required track realignments, rail and tie changes and ballasting. Not much changed the routine at the south rim of the Grand Canyon. The Park Service added new public facilities and roads from time to time as the need arose but the AT&SF and Harvey companies continued business as usual until 1954. At this time Santa Fe management decided to get out of the hotel business at the Grand Canyon. This decision resulted in the sale of all existing commercial facilities to Harvey and the donation of the power house, utility systems and water systems to the National Park Service. The only major changes after the sale occurred when the Harvey Company built a couple of motor hotels that still draw criticism for their modern style, and when they came under the control of AMFAC (American Factors) in 1968.

With this sale an era came to an end. The Santa Fe still owned the right-of-way and the station facilities at the Grand Canyon but it no longer held an interest in the hotel business. Passenger revenues steadily declined but they still continued to advertise the Park as a primary attraction with changes in train service.

Cash transport is one service that did not change as long as the trains continued to run. Until very recently, Grand Canyon Village did not have a bank. As considerable cash is taken in during the course of the day at all of the Harvey-run facilities, the Santa Fe devised a means of handling it safely and securely. At the end of the day, the accounting office, located downstairs in the El Tovar, totaled up the cash, carried it to the Santa Fe cashier at the station and traded it in for an American Express Traveler's Check. This check usually amounted to something in the neighborhood of $25,000 to $30,000 during the summer months of the 1950s. The cashier placed the cash, which included bags of silver dollars brought by dudes from Las Vegas, in the safe at the station until the train left that evening. Just prior to train departure the baggageman signed for the cash and locked it in a special container on the baggage car. Never in all of the years the Santa Fe transferred cash from the Grand Canyon to Los Angeles did a loss occur. No "great train robberies" nor even an attempt to hijack one of these shipments materialized.

What can best describe the relationship of the Santa Fe to the Grand Canyon? Maybe this: Veni, vidi, vici. I came, I saw, I conquered. Add appropriately; I built. Now it is up to us to preserve this architectural legacy. The Grand Canyon Village Historic District helps to insure these monuments to another time will not escape us. This Park Service district contains the older buildings of the Village which will remain as unchanged as possible. Their preservation guarantees us and our descendents a window to the past. It is a remarkable window. Come and enjoy the view.

LOGGING AT APEX

Lumber has been one of Arizona's primary industries for many a year. Most people think of Arizona as one vast desert wasteland. This is hardly the case as the world's largest stand of Ponderosa pine prospers within the confines of the state. A diagonal slash of these great trees stretches across Arizona from the south rim of the Grand Canyon southwest along the Mongollon Rim to the New Mexico border. Williams sits smack in the middle of this beautiful forest. The Grand Canyon Railway runs in and out of stands of Ponderosas at either end of its run from Williams to the Canyon.

Railroads have always needed timber. As surely as trains run on steel they also run on timber. A thirty-nine foot rail requires twenty-five ties to support it. Depending on the method of preservation, its location and the loads carried on the line, a tie can be expected to last from five to twenty years in normal service.

Part of an article in the 16 May 1903 issue of the *Williams News* stated: "It has been ascertained that each mile of the 250,000 miles of railway in the United States requires 400 ties per year. It takes fifty years to grow a tree that will make three ties, and ordinarily requires twenty-five acres to furnish 400 ties." The larger Ponderosas in Arizona could easily do better than this.

With this in mind, The Saginaw Lumber Company of Saginaw, Michigan came to Williams. On 14 February 1893, the company secured timber rights in what is now the South Kaibab National Forest. They wasted no time for they had a lumber mill

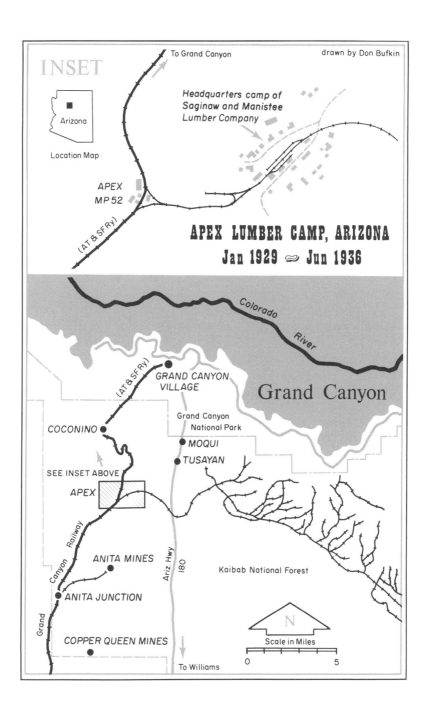

INSET

Arizona

Location Map

To Grand Canyon

drawn by Don Bufkin

Headquarters camp of
Saginaw and Manistee
Lumber Company

APEX
MP 52

(AT & SF Ry)

APEX LUMBER CAMP, ARIZONA
Jan 1929 ⁓ Jun 1936

Colorado River

(AT & SF Ry)

GRAND CANYON
VILLAGE

Grand Canyon

Grand Canyon
National Park

COCONINO

MOQUI

TUSAYAN

SEE INSET ABOVE

APEX

Grand Canyon Railway

ANITA MINES

Ariz. Hwy 180

Kaibab National Forest

ANITA JUNCTION

N

Scale in Miles

COPPER QUEEN MINES

0   5

To Williams

under construction in April of 1893 and in operation by June of that year. These hardy logging Swedes of Michigan brought their particular brand of hard work with them.

Business boomed for them with lumber in demand by local Williams businesses, ranchers and the railroad. They arrived eleven years after the Atlantic and Pacific Railroad's transit across the high desert of Northern Arizona. Continued construction on the new roadbed demanded thousands of ties which Saginaw readily provided.

These industrious people, not content with supplying ties and lumber, built and opened a box factory adjacent to the mill in January of 1894 and this plant provided boxes of every shape and size. The expanding farm industry in the valleys to the south around Phoenix provided their primary business with their increasing need for produce shooks. Fire leveled the factory in June, 1897 but the company rebuilt in very short order.

The Saginaw's primary timber leases lay in the areas south of Williams. Loggers worked these stands with the fervor of beavers and the evidence of their work is still with us in the form of abandoned logging railroad grades which became the forest service roads that give us access to these magnificent woodlands.

Business was good. Good enough that Saginaw decided to expand its operations. This required additional capital and the Manistee Lumber Company of Manistee, Michigan became a willing partner. The merger of these two logging and lumber concerns created the Saginaw and Manistee Lumber Company of Arizona in 1899.

The mill's location in Williams made it very convenient for this company to supply the ties and lumber needs of the Santa Fe and Grand Canyon Railroad during construction. In later years reconstruction of the Grand Canyon line and the heavy requirements for ties by the Santa Fe again caused the company to expand the mill facilities. This mill provided up to five million ties per year to fill the railroad's requirements. Mining timbers for the mines at Anita and other claims in the Francis district also came from this mill. During the building boom at Grand Canyon Village the Saginaw and Manistee also supplied most of the construction lumber for the hotels and buildings. The lumber company therefore became tied to the railroad from its beginnings. Although the mill provided material for construction and maintenance of the railroad at the outset, Saginaw and Manistee did not use the Grand Canyon line for shipment of logs for nearly another three decades.

Forest Service timber leases determined company

Saginaw & Manistee Lumber Company mill and box plant in Williams.
Forest Service

logging operations. Areas south of Williams and in the Chalender and Garland Prairie districts continued to be logged in the Kaibab National Forest. The company also held the leases for the Bellemont district of the Coconino National Forest which they logged in the 1920s. All of these areas are between Williams and Flagstaff.

These Swedes were an efficient bunch. So efficient in fact, they finished these leases in less than thirty years. Not that they destroyed the forest, but the loggers had cut their allotted timber very systematically and the mill and box plant had also kept up with the demands of their customers in the same fashion. The Saginaw and Manistee needed a new lease on life—a new timber lease on life.

New breath came from the Kaibab National Forest in what is now called the Tusayan District. During the early 1900s the Forest Service referred to this area as the Anita-Moqui and later on Grand Canyon District. On 2 August 1928, after the granting of timber rights, the Saginaw and Manistee Lumber Company contracted with the Atchison, Topeka and Santa Fe Railway Company for grading of tracks and sidings at Apex and for rental of 56 pound relay rail.

Construction began on a wye with a 27 car north leg, a 58 car south leg and a 27 car siding on the south leg. They built the turnouts in conjunction with the existing 31 car siding on the east side of the main line. Eventually, this wye fed into twenty six

Williams, Arizona in the 1950s. The Santa Fe yards are in the foreground with the roundhouse (lower r.) and the Saginaw & Manistee mill and box plant (r. center).   Arizona State Archives

miles of main line and spur track to the east of Apex and just to the south of the Grand Canyon National Park. More importantly, it led to a community of people that lived, grew, worked and moved with the job of cutting logs. About one mile east of Apex the company located the headquarters camp for the Saginaw and Manistee operations in a small valley and on the east and west slopes of that valley.

Virtually everything that became a part of this community arrived by rail from Bellemont and Garland Prairie. Housing for the single men looked like small, wooden box cars without wheels. Workers loaded two of these on flat cars or one to a log car for transportation to end-of-track where they established the logging camps. The company provided management and the families with larger housing. Arvid Anderson, the camp superintendent, had the largest house consisting of a living room, kitchen and two bedrooms. Family housing included a living room, kitchen and one bedroom. All of these homes sat on temporary wooden and stone foundations still visible today. One unique feature of these houses is that they came apart at the middle for transport and workers rejoined them in their original "L" or "T" configuration at the destination. These truly "mobile" homes provided reasonably comfortable living for their occupants.

Five houses on the west slope and five more on the east slope made up the initial living quarters of the headquarters camp. Several sheds and buildings for working on the locomotives and other company business occupied positions in the valley by the tracks. Spurs along the valley allowed for the spotting of the commissary car, kitchen and dining cars and the supervisor's car from time to time as needed. Usually they traveled with the loggers to the end-of-track. Two oil tanks and a water tank on the west slope serviced the locomotives.

A gravity feed line from a siding between Apex on the railroad and the headquarters camp supplied drinking water for the camp. The Santa Fe spotted water tank cars there and hooked them up to the water line.

Primarily used for the work train, the longest of two spurs located in the valley occupied the west side of the main logging line. Built for a seven car capacity this track had its turnout at the north end. A shorter spur on the east side with room for two locomotives and tenders had its turnout on the south end. This spur contained a pit for doing maintenance on the underside of the locomotives. The wye at the south end of the camp enabled locomotives to turn around without making the trip up to the Santa Fe siding at Apex.

Logging families included children and they needed an education. An education requires a school and teachers. It mattered little to these people that they lived in the middle of a forest. Apex was home and that's where school needed to be. In the

Lumberjacks using a two man saw on a Ponderosa pine tree in 1929. Forest Service

The Matson family in front of their movable home at Apex. Mr. Matson operated the steam loader.
Matson Collection

fall of 1929 Apex School District Number 3 opened classes in a box car converted to a one room school house. Margaret Longley from Flagstaff accepted the teacher's position prepared to teach grades one through eight. All of this became her domain for the magnificent sum of $130 per month and board. In 1931 Katherine Shipp, also of Flagstaff, succeeded Margaret for that school year. The following year Rose Wilson came from "back east" to teach in the northern wilds of Arizona. The climate must have been agreeable as she stayed until the school closed in the spring of 1936.

Rose Wilson had quite a forceful personality. An excellent teacher, the students remembered her most for her stern and forthright manner. To her, everything had a right way and a wrong way. Ask any of her students and they will tell you her name is Rose B. Wilson. Not Miss Wilson, not Rose Wilson, but most emphatically, Rose B. Wilson. They might have been in the middle of a forest but as far as she was concerned, those children would be taught proper.

Classes never exceeded fifteen pupils but the students rarely filled all eight grades. The school stood above the camp on the west slope of the valley and because of its relatively small size it provided a warm and friendly atmosphere. Students made lasting friendships. For the time this school and its companion school at Anita (District Number 7), were unique in one regard; they were unsegregated. Williams, 45 miles to the south of Anita

Loggers at Apex about 1930. Most of the men pictured here are either Swedish or Swedish-American.　　　　　　　　Matson Collection

Teacher Rose B. Wilson with her class at Apex school about 1934.
Matson Collection

and 52 miles south of Apex, had segregated schools for the Anglos and Mexicans but Apex and Anita schools accepted Mexican and Indian students from the section gangs on the Santa Fe. As the years progressed further into the Depression diversity of the school population would go through quite a few changes.

The Saginaw and Manistee had its origins in Swedish-American culture. Mexicans and others worked in the mill and box plant but in the camps the predominant worker had either been born in Sweden or in the United States of Swedish parents. As time went on Norwegians and Finns began to arrive in the camps. During the thirties hard times prevailed in the midwest. As victims of the dust bowl, Okies, Arkies and Louisianans began their trek to the west in search of work and a better life. All of these good people had been accustomed to hard work but circumstances beyond their control dictated they move on. No strangers to long, hard days they fit into the logging camps very well. Apex became a melting pot. Here a man earned his keep and maintained his self respect while doing an honest day's work for a decent wage and their families met and got to know different kinds of people. Kinds of people they had never had the chance to know before.

Weather permitting, logging continued year-around. Heavy snow falls in some years suspended operations until enough melted away and allowed the lumberjacks to resume cutting. The main line of the Saginaw and Manistee logging railroad at Apex can only be called a dirt track road with temporary spurs to the

Dirt track spur to a cutting area on the Anita-Moqui District. Note the lack of ballast and logs stacked for loading to the left.   Forest Service

cutting areas. Company section gangs normally laid ties directly on the cleared ground without ballast. Stumps of freshly cut trees came up between the ties in many places. The ties came from Santa Fe rejects at the mill in Williams because the company considered the line to be temporary. Ties sank into wet ground and did not provide firm footing for the trains and even when the ground dried out they shifted laterally and the roadbed remained unstable. Enginemen considered this road a real challenge to run.

The hogheads, or as the "real" railroad hogheads called the logging engineers, dinky skinners, had a tougher time of daily operations than did their main line brethren. Usually the locomotive swayed from side to side so badly the crew found it very difficult to maintain balance. Derailments occurred almost daily and usually meant the locomotive got on the ground without rolling over because they operated under reduced speeds as a matter of necessity. These dinky skinners used rerailing frogs as a standard tool of the trade. Most of the time all they needed to get the locomotive back on the track included some rail, frogs and some hard work.

All of the hogheads had come from the old country and still had their Swedish accents. One told the story of a derailment he experienced that summed up his feelings as he recalled the situation many years after it occurred. As the engineer proceeded down the main line light, the locomotive rocked from side to side very badly. When he approached a curve he realized the locomotive would derail so he braked and told the fireman to jump as he thought they might roll over. The other man made it off and when the hoghead tried to join the birds the violent swaying of the engine threw him back into the cab. In the excitement of telling the story his accent came out. "The damn ting was rockin' so bad I yumped twice before I got off the damn ting." Fortunately the locomotive stayed upright and he and the fireman only had some scratches and bruises to show for their flight. Several hours of hard work got it back on the tracks.

The Saginaw and Manistee dinky skinners had three locomotives to work with. Two Baldwin 2-6-0s and a two-truck Shay made up the power roster for the company at Apex. All oil fired, the Baldwins carried numbers 2 and 3 and the Shay number 4. Everyone in the camps referred to them as either the 2, 3 or 4 Spot.

Built in 1904 for the Saginaw and Manistee, number 2 came out of the factory with the name "Aug. Lindstrom" for the company president. Originally numbered 23883 at the factory, it saw extensive use in company operations at Bellemont, Chalender, Garland Prairie and areas south of Williams as well as Apex. The company eventually sold it for scrap during World War II.

Also built for the Saginaw and Manistee, number 3 rolled off the production line in 1907. Numbered 32249 at the factory, it is unknown if it had been named as number 2. The 3 Spot became the backup engine for the Grand Canyon district operations. It also saw service in the other districts logged by the company. When the company completed cutting on the Grand Canyon district in 1936, this locomotive remained on the spur of the headquarters camp at Apex until scrapped in 1941 by Mallin Brothers Scrap Company of Prescott.

Number 4 came to the Saginaw and Manistee in 1923 by way of the Arizona Lumber and Timber Company. Built in 1913 for the Flagstaff Lumber and Manufacturing Company, and numbered 2732 by Lima as a 50-2 class Shay, this locomotive became extensively damaged in a derailment and the FL&M probably sold it to Arizona Lumber and Timber in 1917. The 4 Spot carried AL&T number 7 prior to coming to Saginaw and Manistee. As with the others, it saw service in all of the districts in operation by the company prior to making the trip to the Canyon district. Equiped with gear-driven wheels it had more power than the rod engines and its working environment became the steeper grades and heavier loads the Baldwins couldn't handle. When cutting came to a close at Apex number 4 had also been worn out. The crew spotted her on the water siding at Apex to await the cutting torch

Saginaw and Manistee Lumber Company logging camp number 36 in the Grand Canyon District. Matson Collection

Cat skinner skidding bucked logs to the loading area with the aid of an arch. Forest Service

Saginaw and Manistee Shay 4 spot during loading operations on Skinner Ridge.   Forest Service

in 1941.

Technically it can be said that these three locomotives saw service on the Grand Canyon line but only two made the transit from Williams to Apex and the other one round trip. When they came up the line with the bag and baggage of the Saginaw and Manistee it must have been a sight to behold. Flats with houses followed, along with tanks, log cars with shacks, steam loaders, logging wheels, tractors and the headquarters camp cars. One could almost liken it to a circus train but the Saginaw & Manistee came to Apex for serious business. These people did not represent a traveling circus in any way.

After making the initial move and getting operations underway the daily routine of work became the way of life in the logging camps. Initial cutting headquartered out of Apex and as the cutting progressed east so did the logging camps. They sprang up along the main line and each in turn had to be dismantled when the camp moved. By the time the company suspended cutting operations in 1936 a total of thirty-eight camps had appeared and disappeared.

Apex remained the headquarters and maintenance camp for the duration. All major work on the locomotives, tractors and trucks had to be handled here in the company shops. Hostlers lubricated the locomotives and kept steam up all night long so that they were ready to roll in the morning. If a locomotive spent the night in an advance camp a hostler went with it. Work on the skid cats and trucks had to be completed at night in order for the logging

113

Saginaw and Manistee logging train with 2-6-0 Baldwin 3 spot and steam loader. Forest Service

crews to keep up with cutting schedules. In the winter mechanics drained the radiators every night as they had no anti-freeze. The maintenance men filled them again in the morning and warmed up the engines in time to have them ready to go.

The logging crews' day started at 5:00 AM with breakfast. Felling trees and bucking logs with hand tools caused these men to expend a lot of energy. To replace this energy the men consumed huge amounts of food. Breakfast usually consisted of all they could eat of eggs, bacon, sausage and fried potatoes. Lunch had been prepared and set out for the men to take with them. A usual lunch included four sandwiches of lunch meat, beef or pork, and cake, cookies and fruit. If they wanted more, extra sandwiches could be made by the men from the leftover breakfast bacon and eggs. The kitchen crew always had coffee available and the men left their thermos bottles at the cook shack in the evening for filling in the morning. Cutting crews left for the cutting areas by truck around 6:00 AM and worked until four or five PM with the skid and loading crews usually working for at least another hour.

Another marvelous meal awaited the loggers at dinner. It usually featured meat of some variety (fresh killed deer or elk made the list from time to time) with potatoes, two vegetables, rolls, bread, cake and cookies to top it off. The cooks prepared so much good food for these meals that in a period of five months one commissary clerk ate so much he gained thirty pounds and as a result could barely fit into his wedding suit. Each man in the camp paid for board by having a whopping $1.05 per day deducted from his paycheck. This cost certainly had to be considered reasonable for all a man could eat. In the logging camps meals of this order were a necessity rather than a luxury. Lumberjacks needed every calorie they could get.

The kitchen staff consisted of a cook, dishwasher and two helpers who assisted with the cooking and attended to the serving chores. These men put in extremely long days with their only breaks coming in the morning after breakfast clean-up and on Sunday when their duties required them to serve breakfast and put out lunch meat for the rest of the day.

At Apex lumberjacks used simple tools of the trade. The company provided each man with several crosscut saws and a double bit axe. A lumberjack had to supply his own wooden wedges for felling trees. The company also had a saw filer on the payroll who made daily rounds to sharpen the saws.

Skid crews moved the felled and bucked trees to the loading areas. Cutting crews bucked trees into sixteen foot lengths in this district (other districts used thirty-six foot lengths as their standard), and a choker setter placed a twelve foot cable around the log and attached it to the skid cat (caterpillar tractor) or arch for dragging to the loading area. If the crew had a skid of less than a quarter of a mile they attached the log to the cat and if more they attached it to the arch and raised the front end off of the ground to allow more ease of movement and less damage to the log. In later years trucks came into use in some places to haul the logs to a loading area rather than lay more track or skid long distances.

Once at the loading area loading and train crews took over handling of the logs. Tong hookers hooked up the log to the loader which set it on the car. The Saginaw and Manistee Lumber

Baldwin factory photograph of 2-6-0 locomotive "Aug. Lindstrom." This became the Saginaw and Manistee 2 spot.   Luckeson Collection

Santa Fe double length log cars on the Grand Canyon District.
Forest Service

Santa Fe log train southbound for the mill in Williams.   Forest Service

Company owned the original cars used at the Grand Canyon district which accomodated only one stack of sixteen foot logs. In later years longer cars leased from the Santa Fe held two stacks of sixteen footers.

In order to take advantage of the type of loaders used on this district the loggers cut sixteen foot logs for delivery to the mill. These oil fired steam loaders had small steel flanged wheels which set on tracks on the cars. The tracks came in two sections and made to be picked up and laid down by the loader as it passed from car to car. As the loader operator finished with one car he backed the loader onto the section behind him, picked up the section in front and swung it around to join with the one in the rear. Had it not been for this system they would have used a stationary loader on skids which required the locomotive to move the cars into position for loading. By using this more efficient system the crews no longer had the difficult chore of moving the skid loader to a new site.

Once loaded the logs traveled to the siding at Apex for pickup by the Santa Fe for transport to the mill in Williams. When loads got backed up it is possible they spotted log cars at Hopi siding, two miles south of Apex, for the Santa Fe pickup. The purpose of Hopi has never been clear and this is the only possibility for its use other than as a doubling track. The Santa Fe logging extras brought empty cars from the mill daily and picked up the loaded cars for the trip south. These extras also positioned the cars for unloading at the mill pond as a regular part of the trip. The mill crews rolled two or three logs off into the pond at a time until they emptied the car and the train crew moved the next one into position.

The logging boss's job at Apex required him to act as the field general of the operation and he had a wide assortment of job skills to oversee. His position made him a salaried member of management whereas the company paid the loggers hourly wages. Wages by today's standards seem exceptionally low but the money bought more. For example: a choker setter made about 32 cents per hour; a tong hooker about 38 cents; cat skinners made about 60 cents and the loader operator about 65 cents. Nothing to get rich on but certainly a living wage and during the Depression these men had a job at a time when many others did not. And no matter what the salary amounted to the company usually had a way to get at least some of it back.

The company maintained commissary sold tobacco, canned goods, soap and some other household needs and resupplied it by truck from the commissary in Williams. As usual with company commissaries, they charged prices a bit higher than in the stores. The Saginaw & Manistee payroll department deducted commissary purchases from the wages along with board. Tusayan did not exist and Moqui Camp for tourists did not stock groceries or merchandise so shopping had to be done elsewhere. Occasionally the families or men drove to Williams or the Babbitt store at the Grand Canyon for their shopping needs. Thanks to the Park Service the road to Williams had been paved and except for the dirt roads from the camps to the highway travel to town did not present a problem. At certain times of the year the roads in the forest turn to mud and people in the camps did not consider it unusual to get stuck and spend the night in some abandoned buildings or whatever shelter could be found. During these times the people used the commissary more frequently.

Cooks always kept a fresh supply of meat available for the families. The company stored beef and other meats in a screened in building open to the air. This served as the "cooler." During the winter spoilage did not present a problem but they kept a minimum amount of meat in the summer. Trucks brought more in from Williams as needed. A housewife just went to the cook and purchased whatever cut of meat she needed for that day's meal.

Except for the location family life in the camps compared similarly with family life in Williams. Families which had

Schoolhouse of Apex District No. 3 on the hill above the main camp.
Matson Collection

Rotting ties along the abandoned main line of the S&M logging railroad on the Ten-X ranch.

118

school age children usually lived in the headquarters camp at Apex while those with pre-school or no children moved with the advance camps. Quarters in the camps may have been smaller but many families considered it more convenient to be closer to the work and the commissary car.

Organized entertainment in the camps did not exist. Some families visited each another for relaxation or made a trip to town. Mostly they led a quiet life in the forest and oriented their days about the dictum early to bed and early to rise. Telephones provided the only reliable contact with the outside world. The Grand Canyon line had good communications with telephones at every station. Wires on insulators screwed into live trees ran from this line at Apex to the camps. Poles had been set out by the company only where needed to cross large open meadows. These have all been removed but insulators can still be found in many places today. The caller got the Williams operator to place the call and then disconnect when completed. Much of the time poor connections across the country turned telephone calls into a shouting match but in all probability this still gave the people at Apex a phone system better than most.

"Single" men in the camps had little else but work and an occasional card or crap game to occupy their free time. For some boredom could be relieved in Williams but for most it just wasn't done as many of the "single" men were not single at all.

Santa Fe engineer Sid Terry with the Saginaw and Manistee 3 spot at Apex in 1941. Salvagers cut up the locomotive for scrap at this location.
Matson Collection

These men had families who in most instances lived quite far away and needed the money they earned. Swedes and others had left the old country to make enough money to bring their families over at a later time. Dust bowl victims had been forced to leave their families with what was left of their homes while they searched for work. These separations placed additional strains on the men.

Some men observed an Okie dust-bowler with his head in a rain barrel after receiving a letter informing him he had become a father for the first time. He emerged with a big smile and someone asked him what he had done. "I was jes' listenin' to what 'Pappy, Pappy' sounded like," he replied. A hard working Swede who left his family behind in the old country presented an even sadder situation. Because of the separation he had taken to drinking too much. While in the forest he worked long, hard hours, saved his money and stayed off of the booze. When he saved and/ or borrowed enough to go to Sweden and bring his family back with him he made the trip to Williams to catch the train east but couldn't pass up going into a bar. A few days later he showed up back at camp broke and hung over. This happened several times and it is believed he never made it back to Sweden.

Fortunately, few serious illnesses and injuries happened during these years on the Grand Canyon district. With the nearest hospital in Williams and the nearest doctor only occasionally at the Grand Canyon, anyone seriously ill or injured had a long way to travel for medical attention. Any problem required that the

Stove and wash tub are all that remain of one housewife's kitchen at Apex.

Cross beam of Santa Fe logging car 719 which had been burned but not salvaged at the Saginaw & Manistee headquarters camp at Apex.

Remains of wooden foundation beams for a movable house at the headquarters camp.

stricken individual be placed in a car or truck and hauled to the nearest available treatment. Unless weather presented a problem most people considered it easier and faster to take the patient by vehicle because the scheduled trains on the Santa Fe ran only in the morning and evening.

When 1936 rolled around, the Saginaw & Manistee had nearly completed the timber cutting leases in this district. Two Forest Service men stationed in the camps to mark trees for cutting and scaling (measuring them for board-feet of lumber), finished up their work and went on to other duties. By May of 1936 the last cuts had been made and the final loads left on the Santa Fe for the mill in Williams in June. With no more timber to be cut the logging crews and families moved on to the next lease. This left only the maintenance men and the section gang to start the breakup of the camps and to pull the rail.

The rail remained in good condition so they salvaged it for reuse or resale. Some of this rail might still be in service at the mines around Globe. All of the serviceable rolling stock and the living quarters still in good condition had to be packed up and sent on to the next lease area. Crews either scrapped or burned anything which had become unserviceable or beginning to show its age. They rolled unserviceable log cars with wooden shacks on them into bonfires one after the other. When the fires cooled down the workmen picked up the left over metal for sale as scrap. Classes continued in the school through the spring of 1936 and this caused it to be one of the last buildings moved. When all of the structures and equipment had either been dismantled or sent on to the next lease area the hostlers parked the 3 and 4 Spot locomotives—never to be run again. They met the torch in 1941.

Today, all that remains of a living, vital community are rotting ties, wooden and stone foundations, rusted cans, an old stove and assorted pieces of history. Good memories also remain in the minds of those who once lived in a community with a unique lifestyle. It is a community to be proud of for it brought together in a very difficult time the kinds of people who made this country great. Even now, it feels good to walk in these places and think of them.

PRESIDENTS, KINGS & WORLD CITIZENS: PASSENGERS ALL

When the public learned that the magnificent vistas of the Grand Canyon had been made accessible by comfortable rail transportation they began to come in ever increasing numbers. For many years the more hearty writers who had visited the Canyon during the days of primitive conditions extolled the beauties and unlimited vistas in newspapers around the country. Now, at the behest of the Santa Fe, these writers and others made the trip even more inviting. The railroad's passenger department also generated several publications of their own to further advertise the line.

Dime novels had long since lured easterners with stories of the wild west which more than stretched the truth. When the accounts of the Grand Canyon began to be read side by side with the tales of derring-do in the dime novels, people had to come see for themselves. After all, wasn't it now civilized with a railroad in place? With comfort ensured they now ventured into the wilds of the Arizona Territory in the midst of cowboys and Indians to see this wonder of nature. Oddly enough, many of today's travelers are looking for the same things. This is particularly true of foreign visitors many of whom, via television, believe this is still the Wild West.

Those who were among the first to avail themselves of "civilized" railroad transportation got a little more than they bargained for. Stage coaches remained part of the trip until September 1901. These people got a real taste of the Wild West in

President Theodore Roosevelt addressing the crowd of people assembled at the Grand Canyon for his visit on 6 May 1903.

University of Arizona Special Collections

a dusty, rocking coach ride from Anita Junction at first, and later from Coconino, to the south rim of the Canyon. Certainly it must have been worth it because more and more came to enjoy nature's masterpiece.

In the years to follow people in power positions such as presidents and kings, traveled the railroad right-of-way along with world citizens of virtually every country on the planet. Many came in native costume and some dressed to the nines. All came away duly impressed. Some of the more famous tried to blend in with the people but for many this became an impossible task. Celebrities are usually too easily recognized and world leaders have large security entourages with them. Others played for the press as if on the campaign trail. No matter the status of the individual traveler, the Grand Canyon became a great equalizer. The Canyon could be no more or less spectacular to any of them. It is there and it is overwhelming.

Even one such as John Muir, who had seen the grandeur of Yosemite and the majesty of Alaska, came away impressed even beyond his capacity to describe the Canyon. He had come expecting, as do most conservationists, the worst from man's intrusion upon the scene. His trip in 1902 left him feeling awed with the beauty and expanse of the Canyon and good about man's presence there. He returned several times to take in the

Canyon and to meet twice with Theodore Roosevelt. Both were old allies in the preservation of this country's natural resources. Both traveled the railroad.

Almost certainly President Theodore Roosevelt occupies the position of the most ballyhooed visitor the Canyon ever saw. At the height of his popularity nationally, "Teddy" was a special favorite of almost all Arizonans because of his Rough Rider Regiment. Many of the Arizona men who served in Cuba with him still lived there and some held high positions and all told stories that added to the Roosevelt legend. Advance publicity for his trip to the Canyon appeared in the territorial newspapers for weeks prior to his visit. Along with the usual invitations to dignitaries of the Arizona Territory members of the Rough Riders received special invitations to come have a reunion with their commander.

His visit to the Grand Canyon meant quite a bit to the people of Arizona. Much more than the publicity for tourism was at stake with the Territory of Arizona attempting to become a full-fledged state. Roosevelt held in favor of making Arizona a state but other politics had to be played in Congress. Arizonans figured if they welcomed him just a little bit more energetically than what would be usual he might be persuaded to make more of an effort with Congress. They pulled out all the stops. The Grand Canyon would never see the likes of this visit even when descended upon

Big Jim Gwetva, Supai Indian with his WWI medal from the Queen of Belgium.   Moore Collection

Theodore Roosevelt, John Hance and Emery Kolb & party on the Bright Angel trail in 1911.
National Park Service

by 20,000 Boy Scouts.

Newspapers around the Territory gave almost total coverage to the event. *The Coconino Sun* of Flagstaff printed the president's speech verbatum and the Phoenix newspapers pretty much did the same. Apparently the editor of the *Williams News* became miffed when TR did not stop in Williams, Phoenix, Prescott or Tucson. He printed a story which covered only a quarter column on page two that mentioned Roosevelt visited the Canyon and had been welcomed by several dignitaries. On page one, in an editorial, he belittled Roosevelt for not stopping. It made no difference to him that Phoenix and Prescott are far off the main line and Williams little more than a whistle stop. You can't please everyone!

The Coconino Sun devoted the entire front page of its 9 May 1903 issue to Roosevelt's first visit in Arizona.

PRESIDENT PASSES THROUGH FLAGSTAFF

Flagstaff's Patriotic People Follow Him In Goodly Number To Do Honor to the Nation's Chief Executive—President Presents Diplomas to Flagstaff High School Graduates—The Citizens of Flagstaff Present Beautiful and Costly Navajo Blanket

Wednesday morning [6 May] a large number of Flagstaffians gathered at the railroad station in order to be on hand to take advantage of the necessary stoppage for water,

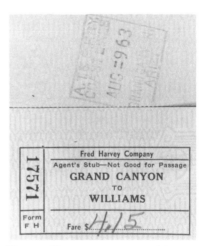

Santa Fe round trip ticket from the Grand Canyon to Williams dated 15 March 1963.

Schmitz Collection

Harvey Company one way ticket from Grand Canyon to Williams dated 9 Aug 1963.

Schmitz Collection

should Mr. Roosevelt arise so early, of catching a glimpse of the nation's well-loved chief magistrate, President Theodore Roosevelt.

At 4:03 a passenger engine drawing six Pullman coaches flashed by the station, seeming to frighten the shadows of the night which seemed adverse to giving way to the just-breaking dawn, back from the railroad into the settled portion of town, to come creeping back again when the engine had replenished its water supply and continued on its way. .... The train carrying the Presidential party continued on without material stoppage to Williams, thence over the Grand Canyon branch, arriving at Bright Angel at 9:30 a. m.

Excursionists from Flagstaff congregated about 5:00 a. m., and an hour later, at 6 o'clock, a train of five cars pulled out from this town bearing 301 enthusiastic people hot on the President's trail.

They were not the only people to run a special this day. A special left from Phoenix "bearing nearly all the territorial officials" and another "carried the Cleveland Greys, the crack military company of the country." The Greys traveled as the official escort of the President. About two hundred people from Williams and a like number from Prescott also came in on a special.

Mr. Roosevelt put in a full day. He said he came to see the Canyon and see it he did. Someone placed a white horse at his disposal and he made good use of it in riding along the south rim. But he couldn't get away from the politikin'. He made a goodly speech about the virtues of the Canyon and praised the railroad for not building anything on the "brink of the canyon." He said, "What you can do is to keep it for your children and your children's children and for all who come after you, as one of the great sights which every American, if he can travel at all, should see."

One boy and four girls, who made up the graduating class of Flagstaff High School, had a tale to tell also. The President personally handed them their diplomas and the Territorial Governor congratulated them. It didn't seem to matter to anyone they "graduated" a month earlier than usual. For the ceremony and to keep the crowds happy that festive day, the band from the Arizona Lumber and Timber Company in Flagstaff had made the trip and played all day long.

Quite a day! The President left the next morning but not before he determined this would not be his last trip to the Canyon. He returned in 1911 and 1913 after he had stepped down from the presidency. No longer required to go through all of the

Locomotives 1370 and 3722 double head El Tovar past Bright Angel overlook at the Grand Canyon on 15 June 1941. El Tovar provided summer passenger service to the Grand Canyon in 1940, 1941, and 1946.
Ingersoll photo, Bassett Collection

El Tovar's eight car consist rests on track 15 at the Grand Canyon station with engine 3854 in the lead. Ingersoll photo, Bassett Collection

hullabaloo on his subsequent trips TR made some extended trips into the Canyon by mule. If nothing else, Roosevelt became one of the Canyon's most exuberant visitors and certainly one of its most ardent admirers.

Although unable to obtain statehood for Arizona (it would not come until 14 February 1912), he continued to be welcome. *The Coconino Sun* of 17 March 1911 had the following two column headline on the occasion of his next trip through:

FLAGSTAFF HEARTILY GREETS ROOSEVELT
People Turn Out Several Hundred Strong to Greet Ex-President As He Passes Through Flagstaff—Remembers His Rough Riders

Theodore Roosevelt might have appeared larger than life to many people but one president who made the trip to the Canyon probably qualified for that title in reality. President William Howard Taft, Roosevelt's handpicked successor, might actually rank as the largest dignitary to ride the rails to the Canyon. At six foot two inches and 355 pounds, President Taft indeed cut an imposing figure. Many stories of his bulk and oversized bathtubs are commonly written about even today. Shortly after taking office in 1909 he and members of his cabinet and staff embarked upon a rail odyssey that covered much of the United States from 15 September to 10 November.

Even by TR's standards this inspection trip of the nation indeed made for a magnificent adventure. It covered 12,759 miles in twenty nine states and two territories (Arizona and New Mexico had not been admitted to the Union at this time). They traveled mostly by rail on twenty five separate railroads but travel by steamer, ferry and riverboat became necessary to visit certain areas. Taft's double headed special had come up from Phoenix via Prescott and Ash Fork. At Williams he made a stop for a speech at 11:25 PM on 13 October. Even at the late hour he drew a large crowd who wanted to hear about statehood. Taft did not disappoint them. Was he not TR's man? After talking with the people he shook hands around and then retired to his "palatial private car." He left Territorial Governor R. E. Sloan, Territorial Secretary G. U. Young and Territorial Representative Ralph Cameron to greet old friends and continue the assurances that statehood would someday be a reality.

Sometime after midnight his train left for the Canyon. According to the *Williams News*, "...the old veteran engineers, Wagner and Lumsden piloted the special train of nine cars to the

Canyon and back. Conductor Duncan was in charge of the train. Fireman Watts was on duty with Engineer Lumsden." They arrived at the rim early the morning of 14 October. It is not recorded at what hour he arose to view the Canyon. As the speech at Williams had been one of 266 he made on this trip and the late hour, it might be assumed he did not see the sun rise.

The Canyon community had prepared for his arrival. Santa Fe crews laid new walks on the El Tovar grounds and the dining room had been outfitted with new tables. Red, white and blue bunting decorated the hotel inside and out. Even a group of twenty-five Indians had practiced diligently to "furnish amusement to the presidential party."

As with Roosevelt the usual dignitaries made their obligatory appearance and many of the visitors who happened to be at the rim paid him attention but no great out-pouring of people came forth to welcome him to the Canyon as had been the case with TR. One might wonder at the thoughts this large man had as to the immensity of the Canyon. In two months time this great man saw and experienced more of this country than the vast majority of its people would in a lifetime. He could have easily by-passed the Canyon but he went miles out of his way to see it. Hopefully he was as impressed as have been the millions of people who followed him.

Taft's train left the Grand Canyon about midnight of

Sam Turner, agent at the Grand Canyon for many years with his wife, Eloise and son, Sam Jr. on the rim of the Canyon in winter.

Turner Collection

130

the 14th. He departed from this grandest of canyons as he arrived—in the dark. He spent all day at the Canyon but saw nothing of the 64 miles between there and Williams. By this time it probably mattered little as he had just barely passed the half-way mark of this marathon rail journey.

The trip to the Canyon by rail became an adventure for everyone whether accomplished in 1901 or 1951. Anticipation of wonderful vistas made the trip an exciting experience. Visitors knew what was to come even if they hadn't been there before—and yet, didn't know what to expect—even if one had been there before.

Although the transfer from the main line to the Grand Canyon line changed in several ways over the years, people always remembered it. Usually passengers arrived at Williams on trains with fanciful names. Scout, California Limited, El Capitan, Super Chief, El Tovar and the Grand Canyon Limited gave the traveler a sense of impending adventure. Santa Fe crews spotted the Pullmans on the Grand Canyon track in Williams and they made up the train for an early morning departure while the passengers slept.

Most Pullman passengers have the memory of being awakened by the porters about dawn. The sun coming over the high country of Arizona in the morning is a sight few people can forget. Then came a mad dash to get washed, dressed and ready for arrival at the Canyon. For those travel-wise individuals who

Two young passengers smile from their Pullman upper berth. A wake up call at sunrise got them ready for the early morning arrival at the Grand Canyon.   Cook Collection

had been up the line before, it became even more urgent to get everything done prior to the horseshoe turns of Coconino Wash because even the most seasoned travelers found it difficult to hold on and shave or brush their teeth while going through the curves. Besides, this fine scenery should not be missed.

For most years, Santa Fe time tables scheduled arrival at the Grand Canyon around 7:00 AM. Easter Sunday became the only exception to this. Sunrise service at the Bright Angel overlook had been the tradition and the train passed right by there. The agent, Sam Turner, requested and got the train rescheduled until after the service had been completed and the choir finished singing.

This early arrival got everyone there in time for a look at the Canyon and breakfast. The engine would pull trains as long as eighteen cars up the grade of the wye and then back down into the station. For a period of time the Albuquerque Division Grand Canyon District time table carried the notation, "No. 14 will turn on wye and back into Grand Canyon." Thankfully no one took this literally and when the train stopped at the depot the passengers stepped out into the crisp, rarified air of the 7000 foot altitude. Harvey buses waited to take them and their baggage to their hotel, with everything cared for without the passenger having to lift a finger. First stop, right up the hill, at El Tovar and for many their first sight of the Canyon. As the bus pulled up and around the loop to the front door, the Canyon dropped off to the right. Such an

Porters assist passengers detraining after their 7:00 AM arrival at the Grand Canyon on 1 Sept 1964. National Park Service

immediate and unexpected introduction usually got people's hearts started, or stopped, as the case may be.

It did not matter if one stayed at the expensive El Tovar or the more moderate Bright Angel, all passengers received the same treatment. Everything necessary had or would be taken care of for the guests by the courteous, efficient Fred Harvey staff until arrival at their room. Then the individual decided to do as much or as little as he wished. Each hotel always had someone ready to help with information or other services if requested.

Fred Harvey buses left on trips to the Watchtower and Hermit's Rest on regular schedules. Drivers, well versed in the history and natural interpretation of one of the world's biggest ditches gave a tour that differed somewhat with the individual. Depending on which driver you had the fortune to be attached to, the Canyon had been dug by either Emery Kolb, Cap Hance or Fred Harvey. The usual story told on Harvey is that he dug it trying to find a nickel he had dropped. Or the one about the Chicago gangster who took one look at the great gorge and turned to his crony and said, "Let's get out of here before they blame this on me!"

Train crews like this hoghead and conductor brought visitors to the Canyon in the early 1900s with ten wheelers like No. 470 of the 468 class.   Ambrose Collection

Around 1911, Harry Adelson (l) shown here with an unknown railroad "bull" served as a regular conductor on the line.

Black Collection

Railroad station people kept busy all day long tending to the traveling needs of the passengers. Tickets had to be sold, telegrams sent, baggage handled, questions answered and problems corrected. Agent Sam Turner always tried to anticipate the needs of passengers and especially those who looked a bit bewildered. One day, as he made his rounds up and down the station prior to the train's departure, he spotted an elderly lady who looked a bit more "lost" than she should. He walked up to her and in his most helpful voice asked, "Ma'am, where are you going?" The reply was quick and direct. "Young man, that's none of your business!" Some days—!

Sam was agent at the Canyon for seventeen years. He, and his wife Eloise, were "family" to employees of the railroad, Fred Harvey and the Park Service people while there. He supervised the functioning of the physical plant and all facilities built by the railroad while a Harvey man managed the hotels. In his capacity many considered him to be the "mayor" of the Grand Canyon Village even if it was under the jurisdiction of the Park Service. He became a part of the Grand Canyon scene and still is in the memory of many people. Sam Turner is still there. On 20 March 1957, he died of a heart attack in their apartment above the station and he rests in the Grand Canyon cemetery.

After 1919 Park Service rangers always attended train arrivals and departures. They answered many of the same questions fielded by the railroad people with the same patience and courtesy. These men and women led interpretive walks and presented talks to visitors on all of the interesting subjects that are a part of the Canyon. Many of these rangers held degrees in geology, biology, anthropology, archaeology and other related subjects. Whatever their background they introduced the visitors to this wonderful place and educated them on its mysteries. Today, interpretive rangers are as much in demand as always.

Over the years the railroad made several changes to Grand Canyon service. Schedule changes coincided with the main line trains. Buses of the Santa Fe Trailways system made runs in the 1930s to the Canyon from Williams in order to accommodate passengers from trains not leaving Pullmans for transfer to the Canyon line. They did so until the Harvey company complained to the Santa Fe about competing with their buses. Santa Fe dropped the service and Harvey buses made all of the normal transfers from then on.

World War II brought on the most dramatic change in service up to that time. The country mobilized for war. The war effort needed railroad equipment. So much so the War Production

Board froze the design of locomotives so only proven models would be produced and time not wasted on development of new equipment. The need of the country and the lack of travel for pleasure during the war eliminated the normal schedule of The Grand Canyon Railway with the exception of the El Tovar and local trains.

On 29 September 1942, crew and station personnel lined up and posed for a photograph by Emery Kolb in front of the "Last Grand Canyon Train." A consist of one coach and a combination baggage/coach car behind engine 1800 made this train usual for the light traffic of the early war years. Certainly not the "last train" but the last to run on the regular Williams-Grand Canyon passenger schedule (trains 14 & 15) until the end of the war.

After the war finally came to an end in 1945, it took a while for the railroads to get back to normal. The heavy demands of the war effort had worn out their equipment. Troops still needed to be moved about the country as several million men and women wanted to get home. And people were not as yet in a frame of mind to do any recreational traveling.

However, on 30 May 1946, the Grand Canyon line opened up for business. Now operating completely under the

Engineer "Dutch" Oswald never missed a chance to mug for the camera with Harvey Girls at the Canyon.   Oswald Collection

Harvey Girls like these three on a locomotive in front of the Williams Harvey House visited the Canyon frequently.   Duffield Collection

Santa Fe banner, two trains steamed into the yards at the Grand Canyon. One special carried Rotary Club members and the local carried freight. Two trains! Not a bad way to open up shop again! Keeping with the custom for specials and the weekly local freight both trains operated as extras. The local made the trip from Williams to the Canyon for many years on Tuesdays but that schedule changed to Wednesdays in 1959. Time tables had not been made up for the Grand Canyon since 1942 and the line operated under that schedule until the new one published in September 1946 came into effect. Trains 14 and 15 made their return to the daily dispatcher's sheet.

     The wartime community at the Grand Canyon had become just another small town with everyone coming closer. During the war very few dudes made their appearance and the only visitors in any numbers came from the desert camps in Arizona and California of the Army Air Corps and field artillery who used the Grand Canyon as an R&R (rest & recreation) camp. Civic organizations met in the El Tovar instead of one of the service or community buildings. Ladies clubs kept busy knitting sweaters and scarves for the troops. Even though they couldn't really get over the shock of the war and the changes it brought to the Canyon, the people who did not go off to war found a new way of life. A quieter way of life. Now, with those two trains back in town, everything slowly changed back to as it had been before the war.

     Specials were back in business. On 3 June 1922

Fred Harvey kitchen staff at the Williams Harvey House made frequent trips to see the Canyon.   Baumgartner-Leonard Collection

twelve specials carrying Shriners and Rotarians strangled the yards at the Canyon when they brought in one hundred twenty-four Pullman cars. In September of 1938, eight specials for the American Legionaires taxed the capacity of the yards. Throughout the 1920s and 1930s specials had been a way of life. Including the local and the regularly scheduled two trains a day, as many as eighteen trains in one day made their way either to or from the Canyon. Shriners, Rotarians, Boy Scouts and football specials for bowl games arrived regularly. Bankers, railroad societies, business groups and organized tours such as Cartan and Cook's Tours made frequent visits. The residents of the Canyon found little difference between the specials of the 1940s and 1950s and those that operated in the 1920s and 1930s.

One thing about specials—they consisted of equipment from all over the country and Canada. When a special rolled in coaches and Pullmans from virtually any rail line in memory made up the consist. Maybe they looked a bit disorganized and certainly not uniform, but everyone definitely considered them colorful.

Not to be outdone by other groups, during June and July of 1950 the Shriners again put into the Canyon in force. On their way to and from Los Angeles, Shriner specials made their stops at the Canyon in a variety of numbers. They equaled the Legion high of eight trains on 18 July. These trains all had double headed steam for power. Who could say diesel power was taking over the railroads? Rose bowl teams made their appearance as did their fans. A Southern Methodist University special made its stop in January 1936. Not to be outdone, the University of Michigan's team, band and supporters brought two trains to the Canyon in January 1951. Again, all steam.

President Roosevelt's visit in 1903 had been spectacular for an organized gathering and for the time brought a very large crowd of people to the Canyon. But the visitation by the Boy Scouts of America in 1953 broke all records and became forever engraved upon the minds of the people who happened to be there in July.

The Boy Scouts had to see the Grand Canyon! Had not TR admonished? "....every American, if he can travel at all, should see." These youngsters had come from every corner of the country and the Canyon is something not to be passed by. The Boy Scouts of America held their annual Jamboree that year at southern California's Irvine Ranch and many of their specials passed right by the Canyon on the way. Scout leaders scheduled stops for all trains, even if only for four hours in some cases.

President William Howard Taft during his visit in 1909 as part of a marathon two month survey of the United States which took him to twenty-nine states and two territories.   National Park Service

Between 12 and 15 July, the first contingents arrived enroute to the Jamboree; and 25 to 28 July saw the remainder on their way home. In these eight days, stopovers had been arranged for four to eight hours. Upwards of 20,000 scouts descended on the facilities like a plague—albeit a reasonably well behaved plague. Souvenirs, sodas and wildlife began to disappear at a phenominal rate. The first stopover shocked the local population. They got better prepared for the second onslaught and still sold everything in sight. Rangers patrolled the station on the lookout for "natural souvenirs" like ground squirrels and in one case, a young fawn. These they returned to the wild.

During these visits, fifty-three specials, all with diesel power, brought in 669 Pullmans, coaches, troop kitchen cars (the Army still had railroad transportation units in 1953 and had made these cars available), and dining cars. On 28 July, equipment taxed the yard limits to capacity when two sections of train No. 14 arrived along with seven scout specials. Nine trains! One hundred and thirteen cars! Two and four unit diesels! Not since 1922 when the Shriners and Rotarians brought in one hundred twenty-four cars had the Canyon seen anything like this.

These trains traveled with ten minutes between sections. With the yard full and visibility next to nothing, some system had to be devised to move these trains safely. For the first time at the Canyon, Santa Fe personnel used radio communica-

Many visitors to the Grand Canyon came to spend some time after having seen the area while in the military. Almost certainly some of these soldiers on this train in front of the Williams Harvey House in 1918 did so. Note the Red Cross ladies passing out treats to the troops and the two soldiers doing guard duty with rifles.   Macauley Collection

tions to get these sections in and out. The line no longer had any block signals. These disappeared sometime in the 1930s. Communications workers and telegraph operators remember standing along the line at key stations to act as manual blocks. In this way, no train moved into a block until the one before had cleared. The whole grand operation never had a hitch. The railroad and the men who worked those days certainly earned a great deal of credit.

Most of the people of world notoriety made their way in and out of the Grand Canyon with little note by the outside world. The local newspapers usually had no comment as the word got to them after the fact. A majority of notices in the papers contained one-liners stating that a certain person had been the guest of the Park Service.

In the late 1940s and 1950s several international visitors made their appearance at the Canyon. Probably King Paul and Queen Frederika of Greece are the most well remembered. "He was tall and good looking and she was gentle" one resident commented about her memories of their visit. They arrived in four special cars for their stay. Dressed in "everyday clothes" they made their way through all of the sights to be seen and then some. On a tour around the Village, the Queen asked to go into the school and speak to the children. Many still remember the day a real

Train crews such as these men brought dignitaries and tourists to the Canyon in the 1910s and 20s.
Oswald Collection

President F. D. Roosevelt with the daughter of Grand Canyon Railway engineer Jack Tooker.
National Park Service

Queen came to school and one lady remembers as a child being patted on the head by the royal hand.

Then came the day His Imperial Majesty, Mohammed Reza Shah Pahlavi, Shahinshah of Iran arrived at the rim. Certainly these better times had to be more appreciated than those he endured in later life. The Shah viewed the Canyon dressed in a business suit with his entourage which included many military men in uniform. Although he required tight security and seldom did anyone smile Dr. Harold Bryant, the Park Superintendent, and Ranger Naturalist Louis Schellbach gave him the complete tour.

Dwight Eisenhower made a quiet visit in 1950 as the guest of Santa Fe President Gurley in his private car. Ike, not as yet President of the United States then held the position as President of Columbia University. Walking around quietly, talking with people and signing autographs, he made no fuss or demands and apparently enjoyed his visit.

Prince Faisal of Saudi Arabia and his retinue of Sheikhs and bodyguards are probably one of the most startling groups to visit the Canyon. Dressed for the most part in Arab costume they presented a sight which caused many visitors to stop and stare. The Ethiopian bodyguards made the biggest impression. Large men by any standards, they were armed with scimitars

140

Military veterans and soldiers on leave at the Canyon form an honor guard during a memorial service for Franklin D. Roosevelt after his death in World War II.   Turner Collection

encrusted with gold and jewels. One lady, invited to tea for the Prince at Dr. Bryant's home, tried to touch a sword and received a most definite, but polite refusal. Tea for a Saudi prince? Certainly! He completed his formal education at Oxford University in England.

One individual, who later served as Superintendent of the Grand Canyon National Park, remembers a wild ride as a boy with Saudis and their flowing robes in a jeep which had been put at their disposal. They used it to travel around to the various overlooks and only seemed to know the location of the accelerator and not the brake. During World War II this same young boy also rode in a tank which belonged to a visiting army unit. Not everyone has memories of riding around the south rim of the Grand Canyon in an army tank or with Saudi princes in a jeep.

The Maharajah and Maharani of Kotah, a state in India, arrived in 1956 along with the flamboyant President Sukarno from the Republic of Indonesia. Quietly, the Maharajah and his family saw the sights and enjoyed the hospitality shown them by the Park Service. Sukarno, with his "uniform" and silver capped swagger stick stood out like a sore thumb and his group always seemed to be quite active. The Village residents quickly noted his eager eye for the Harvey Girls.

Superintendent John McLaughlin gave the King of Nepal and his small group the usual VIP tour of the south rim in

1960 when the King stopped over on his way to the coast from Washington.

Of the "power people," President Theodore Roosevelt made his mark on the Canyon the most indelible. The Canyon drew him here no less than three times and these trips certainly helped to ensure the safety of the natural scene. But he was not the only U.S. President named Roosevelt to make the trip to Arizona's Grand Canyon. TR's cousin, Franklin D. Roosevelt, and his wife Eleanor came this way before the start of World War II. He posed with railroad children and all the while flashed the famous Roosevelt smile.

Celebrities came to the Canyon for relaxation and for work. Many movie, musical, radio and television personalities visited from time to time. Clark Gable, Edgar and Candice Bergen with Charlie McCarthy, Arturo Toscanini, Jimmy Durante, June Lockhart and Doris Day are but a few among the many. Actress Signe Hasse represented her native Sweden. Her comment on seeing the Canyon for the first time, "In Sweden our mountains go up!"

One of the more memorable celebrities was a very heavy set man who weighed too much to ride the Grand Canyon mules. Yet he engraved into the mind's eye of many people the moods of the Grand Canyon and captured forever the pace of the

King Paul and Queen Frederika of Greece with Dr. Bryant in 1953.
National Park Service

President Sukarno of the Republic of Indonesia at the rim in 1956.
National Park Service

142

The Maharajah and Maharani of Kotah, a state in India, and their daughters during their visit in 1956.　　　　　National Park Service

Prince Faisal and Saudi Arabian sheikhs at one of the Canyon overlooks during their visit in 1952.　　　　　National Park Service

Ranger Naturalist Louis Schellbach explaining the topography of the Grand Canyon to the Shah of Iran at a display in the Yavapai Point Museum with Superintendent Bryant looking on. National Park Service

Dr. Bryant pointing out some of the features of the Canyon to the Shah at Yavapai Point.   National Park Service

mules on the Bright Angel Trail. Ferde Grofé wrote the magnificent *Grand Canyon Suite.* A gentle man and very astute, he had the ability to see the sunrises, sunsets and storms of the Canyon and transform them into the beautiful music that should last for centuries. He did not build the Grand Canyon but he allowed us to take it home with us.

Television brought the Canyon into the living room of millions of people. Dozens of documentaries have been filmed for the education and enjoyment of all. One television series actually came to the rim to film one of their episodes and actually tried to fit in with everyone. Small wonder, for it was the always pleasing "Lassie" series. Residents became extras and the Hopi House magically "moved" to Indian Gardens. Cameras can do amazing things. But most of all, the residents remember Jon Provost, the young actor in the series. He fit in with the Canyon children and played with them when not involved in filming. A sudden snow storm provided the excuse for an impromptu snowball fight. Jon became one of the local kids and found himself right in the middle of the winter wonderland conflict.

Lassie presented a different situation. The filming schedule required four "Lassies" to be available at all times. These gentle and well mannered collies had to be kept groomed and clean at all times but they would have been received as wonderful playmates by the Grand Canyon children, who could not keep dogs as pets in the Park. On camera the dogs appeared to be unre-strained but in reality could not run and play like Jon. They resided in one of the Bright Angel cabins during their stay at the rim.

Residents of the Village became avid televison view-ers of the series in order to see themselves in their acting debut. Most found the series to be good for a laugh as they saw themselves and neighbors transformed and as familiar scenes changed names and location to suit the scripts. Maybe there were some who thought—just for a moment—they had a chance to make it to the big time on the magical screen of television.

Dudes came and went. So did the powerful and the glamorous. Residents changed with the seasons and the years. Short and long trains arrived at the depot powered with steam or diesel. But the Grand Canyon of the Colorado was here before and remains. Oh, it changes too. But ever so slowly and slightly. In comparison we, and our history, are here but a second in the time of the earth.

All of us have our own personal reaction to this great and grand canyon. Like the child who asked her father, "what

Dwight D. Eisenhower at the east end of the Grand Canyon yards with Santa Fe president Gurley's private car in 1950.   National Park Service

happened?" If the Canyon could talk, what would it have to say about our comings and goings? Hopefully they would be kind thoughts. Hopefully there will be many more of them yet to come.

ACCIDENTS

People who have spent their working lives with railroads have many good memories. Equipment and other people they worked with evoke stories which tend toward the good times. But occasionally the stories turn to the not-so-good times. Almost everyone who has built a career on the railroad in operations or maintenance of way remembers an accident they had a personal experience with. These accidents involved either themselves, family or friends and are recalled with mixed feelings. These thoughts range from sadness to awe.

Accidents are peculiar phenomena and defined as unintended happenings. No one looks forward to an accident of any kind but when they occur people are drawn to them like magnets. Railroad accidents can be spectacular and many live on in song and legend. Because of their attraction state and county fairs in the early 1900s made them into major events. As if in a Roman arena, crews faced off two obsolete locomotives on a length of track, fired them up and started them toward each other at full throttle. The engineers jumped as soon as they got their hog rolling. The big attraction for the people came from the extraordinary sights and sounds. Anticipation of a corn field meeting, sounds of tearing metal, exploding steam and the inspection of the damage afterwards gave spectators the thrill of a lifetime. Thankfully, as would have been the case in ancient Rome, these exhibitions did not leave any torn or injured people.

In these spectacles, the audience didn't have to experience such a wreck as passengers or crew. No terror, injury or death for them. No clean-up of the torn equipment and track. No rebuilding of the track and repair of the equipment. No payment for the destroyed material. Wrecks on a railroad create complex situations involving many people from the crew and passengers to roadmasters, section gangs, equipment operators, doctors, nurses, administrative personnel and lawyers to name a few.

Some accidents are simple, such as backing over a closed switch or breaking a knuckle coupler. Even these minor incidents require involvement of several people to report, investigate, repair and remedy the situation.

The Grand Canyon line has been remarkably free from accidents compared to the main line. This is attributed to the different style of operations. Main line traffic moves at a higher rate of speed with a much greater volume and tonnage. At most, four scheduled trains a day in each direction made their way along the Canyon road. Usually just one or two made the scheduled run. Some of these trains carried the designation as extras, but at certain times and years they became a regular part of the operations. Also, many specials made their appearance from time to time.

Occasionally traffic on the line gave the impression of being heavy but in reality it was not. The reduced speeds of the many grades and curves also contributed to a lower accident rate. Maintenance of the road by the hard working section gangs and bridge & building crews always kept the line in good condition. And except for the 4-8-4 heavyweights, loads on the tracks never became as severe as those on the main line.

Atchison, Topeka and Santa Fe accident records for the Grand Canyon Railway prior to 1929 do not exist therefore it is difficult to make a complete assessment of the accident trends of steam locomotives for this line. Only a partial comparison can be made of steam and diesel. But apparently diesel operations are safer than steam for a variety of reasons.

The steam locomotive is a large, heavy, fire breathing, steam and cinder belching piece of machinery which gives the appearance of something waiting for the chance to do harm. Many people view it as such, but in reality it is quite innocuous until placed in the hands of man. Then it can be transformed into a people and equipment devouring monster.

Cinders in the eyes and burns from hot metal or steam commonly occurred. Slips from steps or grab irons caused scrapes and bruises usually, and resulted in more serious injuries occasionally. Only infrequently did equipment failure play a part

Wreck of train number 15 at Miller Wash on 29 July 1916. Locomotive 1256 rests on the bridge abutment which collapsed under its weight. Fireman Fred Terry lost his life in this accident.   Black Collection

in accidents and injuries. In the yards at Williams a ruptured steam line blasted one hapless fireman from the cab of the locomotive. He received no burns but broke one leg in the fall.

Long and rigid locomotives obscured the vision of the hoghead when he needed a clear field of vision the most. Because of his position at times he would not be able to see a hand signal given by a brakeman. This could result in backing over a closed switch or moving at the wrong time and breaking a hose connection. The size, weight and weight distribution also made them more prone to getting on the ground by rolling rails on curves if speed was just a bit too much. Flattened wheels, caused by locking the brakes and sliding the engine, commonly appeared in the accident reports. Broken couplers occurred when a hoghead got too heavy a hand on the throttle and didn't take the slack out slowly enough. Many things could go wrong with a steam locomotive but they usually never happened until someone got careless.

Diesels have the same temperament when it comes to accidents as far as being innocuous until the crew gets involved. But diesels create decidedly fewer possibilities for injuries as opposed to steam power. Visibility is considerably better because most units have more forward viewing area and are usually shorter and more flexible. Communications between brakemen and the engineer are better due to this greater visibility and the frequent use of radio communications. Cinders no longer plague crew member's eyes but burns from hot engines happen from time

Wrecker and bridge & building crews clean up the damage caused by the washout which destroyed the bridge and abutments.   Oswald Collection

to time. With a little ingenuity crews are still able to find ways to break hose connections and knuckles, back over closed switches and flatten a wheel or two. A moment's inattention also gives someone the opportunity to slip from steps or grab irons and ding their anatomy.

Diesels did have the uncontested edge on safety in the major accident category. No major derailments or deaths on the Grand Canyon line involving diesel equipment could be found in the record. Sadly, this is not the case for steam.

During construction of the line a fair number of accidents probably occurred but to date no reports of incidents have been found. If anything got on the ground at that time it might have gone unreported just for good public and corporate relations.

The first known locomotive derailment cannot be documented with records but the information comes from what should be a reliable source. This incident was not an accident either. Two young brothers, looking for some mischief one summer day in 1902, found more than several people would care for, including themselves.

As they wandered near the yard limits on the north side of Williams, they threw an unlocked stub switch off the main line of the Grand Canyon road and hid in the sunflowers hoping to watch the returning train jam on the brakes and listen to the crew cuss. Trouble was, by the time the hoghead saw the open turnout, it was too late. Engine 282, the first scheduled locomotive to the

150

Canyon, went in the ditch and rolled over. While it lay there "belly up" with the bell ringing, the scared boys ran for home. Luckily, no one received any serious injuries and probably some unknown, 'dumb' brakeman got the blame for leaving the switch open. Apparently 282 did not sustain much damage for it remained in service until 1905 when the Santa Fe sold it for scrap.

Two unusual points relate to this story. The boys never mentioned this story to anyone until after one had died and the other was close to finishing out his retirement from a long and illustrious career. That brings us to the other unusual point. For many years he held the number one position as senior engineer for the Santa Fe and he ran the Super Chief through Williams. How many times did he wonder as he sped down the tracks, "Are there any boys out there leaving a switch open for me?" As best is known, he finished his career on the Santa Fe with a very admirable accident record and never went in the ditch.

About the time this last incident happened is when accidents along the Grand Canyon line started making the news. The first of these, and only the more serious ones will be covered in this record.

The 27 September 1902 issue of the *Williams News* reported the accident which caused the first fatality. Cattle and sheep always presented a hazard along this line and hardly a week went by without several being struck. In this instance, the consequences became far more serious.

Wreck on Canyon Railroad
Work Train Derailed By a Band of Sheep—One Man Killed

A backing train, a cut on a curve with a heavy down grade, a large band of sheep and an excited herder resulted in a wrecked train, the loss of one life and a number of men being badly injured on the Canyon railroad, about four miles north of Williams, last Saturday [20 September] afternoon.

A work crew consisting of the foreman and eleven men had been waiting on a siding for the scheduled train to pass by. When they got underway the caboose with all of the crew aboard actually headed up the work train as it backed up the track toward their destination. Just before the point of the accident the train passed through a deep cut. When they came out of the cut on to a sharp curve a large band of sheep in charge of a Mexican herder had begun to cross the tracks and now confronted the speeding train.

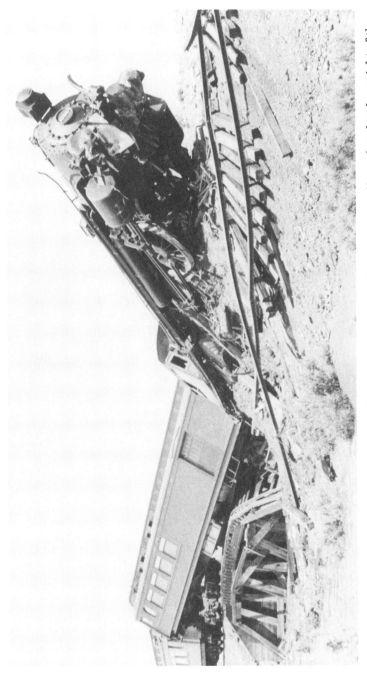

Engine 1256 in the ditch the day after the accident. Note how the bridge abutment collapsed under the weight of the locomotive and the tracks displaced by the flood waters.

Black Collection

Conductor J. O. Dodge and brakeman E. S. McClure were in the cupola. One of the workmen hollered, "Look out! we are going to get into it." McClure applied the air in the caboose and Dodge signaled the engineer. Too late! The caboose plowed into the sheep and as they piled up under the wheels it derailed and rolled over down the embankment trapping the crew in or under the car. Fortunately the locomotive remained on the tracks which allowed the engineer to beat a hasty return to Williams for help. Dr. Tyroler and workmen with tools boarded a car for the ride out to the wreck. The doctor treated almost all of the men aboard the wrecked caboose for injuries ranging from minor to serious.

One individual could not be helped. While the injured received medical attention crews worked to retrieve one man's body from under the shattered caboose. After the injured had been given all of the treatment possible at the scene they loaded them on board the train for the return trip to Williams and further medical care. Their friend's body accompanied them on the journey to town. Follow-up stories reported the coroner's inquest which levied no blame in the accident for the death of the workman, P. H. Swan, as this is open range. The railroad returned Swan's body to his family home in St. Louis in the company of a fireman from Winslow.

Newspaper stories did not seem to follow any particular format or priorities for the reporting of accidents. The story above had a two column headline, probably due to the unfortunate death of Mr. Swan. Editors banished accounts of other accidents of at least equal interest to the interior pages with no headline whatsoever. Witness the following story about a wreck and an engineer being trapped for twelve hours under his locomotive in the 27 September 1903 issue. It had been buried on the third page along with advertisements and local stories of who was traveling where.

Quite a serious wreck occured about 9:30 Wednesday evening [23 September] on the Canyon road out near Anita. Heavy floods had washed away portions of the track and a special train pulled by Engineer Siegendaller ran into one of the washouts in the dark. The engine was overturned, pinning the engineer underneath, where he remained about twelve hours before he could be extricated. He was badly scalded and bruised up. Dr. Tyroler was summoned and went out from here on a special, but on account of the washouts on this side of the wreck he had to cover about eight miles on foot. Yesterday afternoon about four o'clock the delayed train arrived, bearing a large crowd of passengers and the injured engineer. His condition is not considered dangerous. The news of the washout was carried to Bright Angel—a distance of twenty miles—by a young man, one of the passengers, who reached there about four o'clock a.m.

Here is the sum total of the story as reported. Nothing further on the engineer or the young man who made a great effort in getting the news to the Grand Canyon. His trek of twenty miles in the dark walking on a road bed difficult to negotiate due to lack of ballast surely should have received a bit more attention than that. Engineer Siegendaller probably appreciated his efforts more than anyone else.

Then in the issue of 7 May 1904, the *Williams News* reported the following story in two column headlines.

Wreck On Canyon Road
Regular Train Ditched Sunday by Broken Rail

Last Sunday [1 May] the regular Grand Canyon train was derailed a mile north of Valle, thirty miles from Williams. The accident was caused by a broken rail, and from the manner in which the engine, tender, two water cars and the combination baggage and smoking car bumped over the ties through a cut it is miraculous that no serious damage re-

Elk's special on the ground at MP 13. Accident on 11 July 1906 was caused by the spreading of the rails when the roadbed got soft from heavy rains. Note the passenger coaches passing on the shoofly and the extra water car on the special.   U.S. Geological Survey

Log train wreck in 1916 with conductor Harlie M. Goss standing on top of the uppermost log.   Black Collection

sulted and that no one was injured.

The accident happened, too, in the midst of the heavy traffic to the coast of easterners bound for Los Angeles to attend the Methodist conference, and a number of special trains were delayed many hours before the road was cleared.

The editor apparently decided the importance given a story based on his own personal priorities and how slow the news was that particular week. But usually, the news appeared in the correct context for many stories like the following in the issue of 4 February 1905 got short mention. "About 3 a.m. Monday morning [30 January] train No. 14 on the Canyon road, ran over and killed twenty-seven sheep belonging to Charles Howard."

During the early years of the line, the terrible condition of the roadbed plagued the railroad constantly and it is certain far more derailments occurred than made the newspaper. In actuality the line had nothing more than a dirt track railroad with little or no ballasting. All of these accidents most likely became the moving force that got the railroad overhauled and literally rebuilt in 1907 and 1908.

The next two stories in the *Williams News* pointed up the terrible condition of the roadbed and the delays and inconvenience to passengers caused by the lack of sound tracks. Accounts of accidents suffered by a work train and a special point directly to the poor state of the right-of-way. Issues of 4 March 1905 and 14

155

Trainmen pose with wrecked log train near the Saginaw and Manistee mill on 30 July 1916. A broken rail caused the wreck.

July 1906 respectively had the following stories:

> Last Sunday morning [26 February] Gallagher's work train on the Canyon road with Conductor Hogue in charge, went in the ditch at Twin Bridges, about twelve miles north of Williams. The tender, tie car, water car and commissary car were thrown from the track but no one was injured. The accident prevented the passenger train from getting through Sunday, but the passengers were transferred to a train sent out from here, and arrived some hours later. The roadbed is very soft from the recent storms, and although every precaution is being taken, accidents of this kind are liable to occur in spite of them. The track was repaired so as to allow trains to run on time Tuesday night but are not allowed to run on schedule time.

> Elk's Train Wrecked
> Last Wednesday afternoon [11 July] two special trains arrived here from Los Angeles, bearing the California delegation of Elks to Denver. The first section, leaving here at 3:30, was wrecked thirteen miles out on the Canyon road, the accident being due to the spreading of the rails. However, no one on the train was injured, though two of the Pullmans were derailed and some four hundred feet of the track torn up.

The passengers were transferred to the regular train and taken on to the Canyon, where a banquet and a grand ball was held later in the El Tovar. All other traffic was delayed till Thursday morning. The Elks returned to Williams that afternoon and continued on east.

Storms and poor construction by the original builders seemed to be the nemesis of the Grand Canyon line in these years before the Santa Fe decided to totally rebuild the right-of-way. Even after the overhaul Mother Nature had a way of cancelling out all of the hard work. On 29 July 1916, tremendous thunder storms had delayed traffic on the line all day. A two car passenger train at the Canyon had been sitting out the storms for a couple of hours when engineer "Dutch" Oswald and fireman Fred Terry decided the time had come to give it a try. The *Williams News* on 3 August gave the following report:

Cloud-Burst Causes Canyon Road Wreck
Fireman Fred Terry Loses His Life—4000 feet of Track washed out

As the evening train on the Canyon road was making the run from Grand Canyon to Williams last Saturday night it ran into a flood between Anita and Willaha which had been caused by a cloud-burst. The speed of the train was slackened and engineer W. E. Oswald felt his way along, but on reaching and entering upon a bridge over Red Horse Wash the engine went down taking engineer Oswald with it and fastening fireman Fred Terry between engine and tender. Engineer Oswald escaped from the wreck without serious injury but before fireman Terry could be released he was enveloped in steam from a bursting pipe and scalded to death.

The storm deposited tons of rain and hail in the drainage which crossed under the railroad. When flood waters reached the bridges spanning the wash hail began to pile up around the abutments and pilings and formed a dam. Backed up water flowed over the tracks and around the bridges. Ballast and tracks washed away along with several bridges. When engineer Oswald eased out on to the bridge the abutments no longer had the strength to support the weight of the locomotive and it came crashing down.

Several follow-up articles appeared with eulogies for Fred Terry and accounts of his funeral. Out of consideration for the family the *News* did not report Terry's death had been long and

Conductor Harlie M. Goss in his Santa Fe passenger uniform about 1928. Goss died when he fell under the wheels of his log train in 1935.

Black Collection

painful in coming. Consequently nothing could be reported about how much Oswald had tried to help Terry. Oswald lost several toes to frostbite from standing for many hours in the hail while he attempted to comfort Terry. He did die before a doctor arrived and the crew packed his body in some of the hail piled up around the bridge to keep it in a better condition. Another most unusual part of the story also never made print. Prior to leaving the Grand Canyon, Terry told Oswald he had a premonition about that night. He said, "I know I'm gonna get it tonight."

Another problem with this story is that the location given in the story is incorrect. In several official and news accounts the location for the accident is given as Red Horse Wash which is between Anita and Willaha. Actually the accident occurred four miles further south at Miller Wash. This is two miles south of Willaha and north of Valle. Santa Fe engineering drawings put the location of the accident at bridge C-36 (now D-36) which today is right at milepost 36. For some reason train and track crews still carry on the misnomer and refer to this as Red Horse Canyon.

In 1916 the line curved heavily through Miller Wash with four bridges to span the turns of the creek. These curves necessitated a considerable reduction of speed even in good weather and today the signboard restricts speed through the wash to 25-20 miles per hour (25 for freight and 20 for passenger). After a realignment in 1931 the line through the wash became relatively straight with only one curve between the third and fourth bridges.

This straightening of the line caused the milepost to be moved about 1/2 mile north from where it was at the time of the accident.

With the curves in place at the time, the speed restrictions and the weather conditions, engineer Oswald must have had the train at a crawl. And yet the momentum of the train was sufficient to carry it over the washed-out abutment onto the partially washed-out road bed. The slow speed is indicated by looking at the photograph and noting very little damage to the combination car which literally dropped into the creek with very little forward momentum.

It appears engineer Oswald had taken reasonable care under the circumstances. Certainly he cannot be faulted for not realizing the potential a major thunderstorm cell holds for disaster. Who would believe such an incredible amount of hail and water could be concentrated in one small drainage? Who indeed would believe the amount of hail necessary to form a dam could be deposited in such a short period of time? An ice dam at bridge C-36 caused the south abutment of the bridge to wash out when the water piled up behind the dam at the spans and flowed over the fill at the abutment.

Although news reports changed the location they did give a reasonably accurate account as to the extent of damage to the roadbed and bridges. Santa Fe engineers made the impres-

Dr. P. A. Melick, Santa Fe physician and surgeon in his office in Williams about 1900. Dr. Melick survived a railroad crossing accident in which his passenger, George Barnes, died in 1926.   Melick Collection

sive final tally. The flood moved one thousand feet of track six to ten feet off of the fill and washed out all of the ballast from milepost thirty-six to bridge C-36, a distance of four thousand feet. Furthermore, the tons of water and ice shifted one of the three bridges out of line and completely destroyed the other two.

Passengers suffered little injury but had to be returned to the Canyon until the following Monday. A train delivered them to the accident site and transportation around the gap brought them to another train which carried them to Williams. The accident at Miller Wash brought out the best in many people. Everyone did their best from engineer Oswald to the hard working crews who literally rebuilt one mile of track and three bridges in one week.

An automobile accident at a crossing turned out to be one of the more unusual along the line. It involved the Santa Fe doctor from Williams. The following headline appeared in the 15 January 1926 *Williams News* :

George Barnes Killed And Dr. Melick Seriously Injured In Railroad Crossing Accident

George L. Barnes was Killed almost Instantly and Doctor Melick was Seriously Injured Thursday Morning [14 January] When the Inclosed Car In Which The Men Were

Williams hospital built by Dr. Melick in 1898 in which he treated patients for many years before and after the accident.   Melick Collection

Riding Was Struck By Southbound Grand Canyon Train At
Abra Crossing, Formerly Known As Valle

An early morning rabbit hunting trip had lured
Barnes and Melick to the Cataract Creek country west of Valle.
The crossing at Valle station made for the quickest and best way
to the "Island" country. With Dr. Melick's Maxwell closed up to the
cold they approached the crossing from along the stock yards and
never heard or saw the train until it was too late. George Barnes
saw the train first. He yelled, "Train Doc!" and attempted to jump
but the train hit them before he could get clear. When the engine
hit the car the right side caved in and this is what saved Doctor
Melick's life. Barnes, thrown from the vehicle, came to rest in a
rock pile. The crew found Melick near a telegraph pole with the car
on top of him. Directly above him the bashed-in side of the car
protected him from further injury.

Because of the obstruction posed by the stockyards
neither the occupants of the car nor the crew of the locomotive saw
the other until the car arrived on the tracks about one hundred feet
in front of the train. Impact occurred even before the brakes could
be applied. When the train finally stopped the trainmen raced
back to the crossing. Barnes could not be helped but the crew
removed Melick from under the wrecked car and treated him as
best as they could. The trainmen loaded Barnes's body and Doctor
Melick into the baggage car and brought them into Williams.

Further newspaper articles eulogized George Barnes
and gave accounts of Dr. Melick's progress. He did remain
unconscious for about two weeks after the accident but survived
and regained most of his mobility. Melick never completely recovered from the injuries suffered in the accident but he did return to
medical practice and lived to help many of his fellow Williams
residents.

A veteran conductor for the Santa Fe who worked on
both passenger and log trains did not fare as well. He met his fate
while working on the log trains he preferred over passenger
service. On 20 June 1935 Harlie M. Goss fell to his death as his
train passed in front of the Fray Marcos Hotel. The account of the
accident appeared in the 21 June issue of the *Williams News*.

Tragic Death Meets Railroader
Harley [sic] M. Goss, 51 year old pioneer Northern
Arizona Railroad conductor, was instantly killed at 4:45
o'clock Thursday afternoon when he fell into the path of the
slow moving log train. The wheels passed over one leg

Engine 3853 rests on the Kaibab limestone of Tooker Cut the day after the accident while supervisors try to decide how best to remove the wreckage.
National Park Service

Santa Fe wrecker from Needles preparing to lift 3853 back onto the rails on 28 July. Crews did a remarkable job of clearing this wreck in three days.
Moore Collection

A case of backing the train too far in the Grand Canyon yards.

National Park Service

through the pelvic bone and hip, bringing instant death.

Delivery of log cars to the Saginaw and Manistee mill pond on the southwest side of town necessitated backing the train down to their siding. The locomotive pushed the train from the rear with Goss occupying his usual position on the front of the lead log car. When the car had reached a position in front of the ticket office witnesses observed Goss climbing up on the logs in an apparent attempt to signal the engineer. He fell from the top of the log stack in such a manner that no one could determine the reason. The witnesses reported seeing him "straighten up and then throw his arms upward and fall."

Goss became the last person to suffer a fatal accident on the Grand Canyon line. He had survived the Spanish American War and several derailments in the past but did not escape from this one. It is thought he suffered a heart attack and this is what caused his fall. The people of Williams and the Grand Canyon held him in high regard and eulogies gave glowing accounts of his history and contributions to the communities and the railroad.

One last major accident waited in the wings. On 27 July 1939, a special entered "Tooker's Cut" at the north end of Coconino Wash a bit too fast for the curve and got on the ground. Actually, it got on the wall. The 3 August issue of the *Williams News* carried the following account:

163

Wreckage Cleared, Service Resumed On G. C. Railway

At eight o'clock last Thursday night a special Santa Fe passenger train carrying tourists from the Grand Canyon was wrecked in a 'cut' about eight miles south of that city on the Grand Canyon Railway. The train was a double-header and the two engines left the rails on a curve in the cut, lodging up against the solid stone embankment on the outside of the curve. The combination baggage and bar car followed the engines and lodged against the embankment, but the car behind it broke loose, turned at right angles to the track leaped the embankment and took out across country for several yards before it came to a halt still standing on its wheels. The next coach followed after the engines while the rest of the train remained on the tracks.

Another special following about ten minutes behind could have plowed into the wreckage even with the reported brilliant moonlight as there had been no time to set out warning flares. The hoghead (whose name did not appear in the reports) averted what could have been a real tragedy when he saw the rising steam and recognized it for what it represented. Had the boilers been punctured as reported there probably would have been an explosion with loss of life. Actually, the rising steam came from ruptured cylinders which had been broken open on the limestone wall.

Reports told of engineer Sparks, despite his own "severe" injuries, refusing to leave the accident site until all passengers had been accounted for, calmed and given first aid. Fifty-one people had been injured, five seriously. Ambulances took the people with serious injuries to the Grand Canyon and the remainder of the passengers boarded the other special for the return trip.

The accident occurred at a rather difficult location and to clear it required a wrecker from Winslow and another from Needles. Maintenance of way supervisors made original estimates of several days to a week for removal of the wreckage and track restoration but crews working furiously cleared the tracks and in three days scheduled service resumed. Not including transportation costs, lost revenues, medical expenses and settlements from lawsuits, the cost to the Santa Fe for damage and repairs amounted to $51,701.74.

Williams station became a madhouse the day after the accident when a fleet of forty Fred Harvey and Santa Fe

164

Trailways buses brought all of the passengers from the two specials into town. The baggage had to be brought in on another fleet of rented trucks as the buses did not have enough room.

Nothing is ever simple or glamorous about railroad accidents but they are certainly spectacular. Occasionally the memory of taking care of one under trying circumstances allows the participant a bit of a chuckle.

When one of the heavy 2900s got on the ground at the Grand Canyon, Roadmaster M. E. Spivey arrived to find the huge machine, the crew and the section gang all awaiting his instructions. To add to his problems he had an "audience" of Santa Fe management people giving him and the engineer advice on how to solve the problem and get the locomotive back on the track. Spivey had considerable experience with this situation and went about his business.

He put his section gang to work lining up spare track, ties, tie plates and frogs to his satisfaction while ignoring the interruptions of 'armchair' management. After getting everything set he told everyone to back off and went to talk to the engineer. He asked, "Who's the boss here?" The hoghead came back with a direct, "You are, Mr. Spivey." "Good!" he said, "Just remember that and pay no attention to those other people over there." referring to the management men. "Just put the power to her and keep her going until I tell you to stop."

Spivey had orchestrated this concert. He took the position of maestro at the podium and raised his arms. The engineer sat poised with his hand on the throttle of his 975,400 pound instrument. Critics in the form of Santa Fe 'brass' awaited their chance to offer unwanted advice or to say "I told you so" in order to show their superiority. Swinging his arm Spivey gave the engineer the highball and the concert was on! Immediately tie plates and ties began to fly in all directions as the tremendous weight of the 2900 and its tender brought to bear 66,000 pounds of tractive force from the drivers. The 'brass' began to scream and holler for the engineer to stop but he kept on going with Spivey giving him the go-ahead. In a matter of a few seconds the huge locomotive sat on the tracks in fine condition. With only the light 'panting' sounds of the steam passing through the valves the locomotive gave the impression of a huge puppy quite pleased with itself. The only casualties were the red-faced 'brass'. When a concert is well planned and orchestrated the music is sweet.

STEAM & DIESEL: THE POWER

History, tradition, scenic rides and a sense of nostalgia for things past attract people to railroads. But when asked to single out any one thing as a reason for their interest the overwhelming vote is for the locomotives. Why? Probably because of the raw power exuded even as they stand still. Rhythmic pumping and gentle hissing of steam give rise to the frequently expressed idea that a steam locomotive is breathing. Earth shaking rumbles from a parked diesel give the impression of a wild animal waiting to charge. When first approached, a locomotive does not give the impression of a large inert piece of machinery but rather something alive and something a person can get to know and become attached to. Power has a way of attracting people. When people can harness and control that power it becomes even more attractive.

Steam and diesel locomotives have their proponents and both deceive the casual observer. Hardly anything appears more complex than a steam locomotive. Yet, it operates under basically simple principles. They are intricately constructed but the technology is basically simple. Diesels appear to be quite simple but in reality are quite complex. Imagine being able to be the master of something as complex and intricate as a locomotive. Design and operation of such a wonder is beyond the dreams of most people. But to know that other human beings build and operate them is a heady thought.

Locomotives in motion epitomize power, control and

Pages from Fireman S. E. Creel's
timebook dated September 1929.
Note Grand Canyon (GC) entries.
Schmitz Collection

Cover of Engineer E. L. Schmitz's
Santa Fe rulebook number 43438.
Schmitz Collection

RULES AND REGULATIONS

OPERATING DEPARTMENT

grace. They always seem to have the ability to do as they wish, pleasing everyone without opposition. The sight and sounds of a steam locomotive, especially a double-header, working up a grade under a heavy load once experienced is never forgotten. Billows of smoke and steam and the sound of bells, whistles and the thrilling barkin' of a locomotive in full cut-off are the essence of memories. To uninitiated souls these sounds could be disconcerting. The early morning trains pulled into the wye at the Grand Canyon chuffin' and clanging up the grade near the tourist cabins. It was not unusual to see a half awake tourist in his shorts come running out the door of his cabin in a state of mild panic as the locomotive came a barkin' up the wye. Having pulled in the night before he probably wasn't even aware there were any railroad tracks within miles of the place. He should have been up at the rim watching the sunrise anyway.

Many people of the Village looked forward to train arrivals in the morning. As the train backed down the wye the staff of the laundry usually waved it in. After a two hour and fifteen minute pull up the road the crew looked forward to this daily greeting. Grand Canyon Village was home to many of the crew. Children and wives would be waiting for father to come home on the morning train.

Every now and then something a little out of the ordinary happened for these family members to look forward to. One morning a conductor's daughter waited to greet her father as usual along the tail of the wye. As she strained her eyes looking

167

for her dad she looked into the cab of the locomotive. Her father was running the locomotive! The hoghead, who wore a wooden leg, was nowhere to be seen. When her father stopped the train at the station and climbed down from the cab the excited daughter lit into him with a barrage of questions. Why are you running the train? Where is the engineer? To all of this he calmly replied, "He got his leg waterlogged." The fireman just stood there and grinned.

Crews started their day at one or two in the afternoon when they got out of bed and got something to eat. This left a few hours until check-in and they either spent the time with their family or watching the dudes. Mule passengers in the corrals and on the trail provided the most entertainment. Dudes showed up wearing shorts and all sorts of clothing to ride the mules into the Canyon. Wranglers patiently sent them back to their rooms after advising them of the improprieties of their choice.

Most of these dudes had never seen a mule, much less been on one. Almost all of the riders did not have any idea of what to expect for they never had an opportunity to become accustomed to the ways of mules. Embarrassment of some of the ladies always provided some fun when the mules did what came naturally just after starting down the trail. The mules have a regular relief station and the first mule always made his/her stop. Riders screamed and hollered all they wished but the mule did not budge until finished. Some passengers asked the wranglers to make the mule stop doing what had to be done. Much to the further embarrassment of the rider he replied, "Lady, he's doin' jes what you had to do this mornin'." Bad enough for the first rider but the others in line knew what was going to happen next. No help there either. Some passengers even dismounted and walked away until their mount had taken care of business.

After the train pulled into the wye in the morning it then backed into the station for the passengers to offload. Service personnel cleaned the cars (car attendants at Williams did the major clean-up during the night), and performed minor maintenance. Hostlers serviced the engine and filled the tender at the Poage water tower. The Santa Fe never built or even authorized an engine shed at the Canyon. For all of those years hostlers serviced the locomotives in the open with no shelter from the weather. Hostlers and mechanics completed major servicing and maintenance at the roundhouse in Williams. After servicing the locomotive, the hostlers then coupled it to the train and left it to wait for the crew. Steam pressure in the boiler needed to be kept up while the train waited for the return run to Williams. The hostler did this by attaching a steam line from the powerhouse to

Crew and station personnel line up for a photo with engine 1251, a 1226 class 4-6-2 Pacific, with three coaches and a combination car at the Grand Canyon depot about 1915. Note trees between the tracks.

Kolb photo, NAU Special Collections

the locomotive and keeping a low fire in the firebox.

When the crew arrived for the evening train the usual paperwork needed to be done, train orders issued and signed for and the inspection of the equipment. The conductor signed the forms, inspected the cars and got ready to receive the passengers. Hogheads and firemen made sure the motive power had been serviced and they had all of the required safety gear. The brakeman checked the trucks, brakes, air and steam connections and couplers on the cars.

To begin his inspection the fireman climbed up on the tender and checked for a full load of water. He then measured the fuel with a dip stick. The lubricators for the water pump always required a thorough examination. Regulations required certain equipment to be carried at all times. The fireman inventoried these items: two tallow pots of valve oil and engine oil (kept above the firebox to keep it warm), all safety gear such as fusees, torpedoes and the red and white lantern lit and ready, and a spare bucket of anti-foam compound for the water. He then made sure the sand box contained enough for the run and the scoop. Then he went up on top to oil the bell and back into the cab to inspect the firebox for carbon buildup. Too much carbon got a hostler in trouble as his job required him to get it raked out. Last, but not least, he checked the water glass (make sure there were spares),

The railroad and people of Grand Canyon village had strong ties and even today the high school uses an old Santa Fe steam locomotive bell for their victory bell.

170

steam pressure and the injectors.

The hoghead gave the whole locomotive a good going over to make sure everything worked properly. He checked the cylinders and air pumps for leaks and function and then lubricated everything in sight that moved. The engineer needed the old long-stemmed oil can to reach the valve guides, pony trucks, butt ends and the brakes on the tender and drivers. Then he climbed up into the cab to check his valves, injectors and controls. Satisfied that all was well he kicked back and talked with passengers who looked over the engine and asked all sorts of questions about what made it go and why. Making it go is no real problem. Knowing how to make a locomotive do what and when you want it to do is another story entirely. The fireman's job is to provide the steam. The engineer's job is to use it. Together they get the train to its destination.

Some hogheads delighted in giving their firemen a rough time of it. With the Johnson bar in the corner and the throttle wide open a fireman had all he could do to keep water hot much less keep up enough steam. Between exhortations of "Smoke 'er laddy!" and "Kid, you haven't got enough hot water over there to boil eggs on!" the sweat and dirt streaked fireman would be bustin' his chops.

Firemen, especially on the Grand Canyon line, have a real problem keeping water at the correct levels and maintaining the right amount of steam pressure. Keeping track of how much

Fireman Frank Merrifield uses the water column at Grand Canyon to fill the tender before the return run to Williams. The water column was located on the north side of the yards near the old powerhouse.

Merrifield-Rinehart Collection

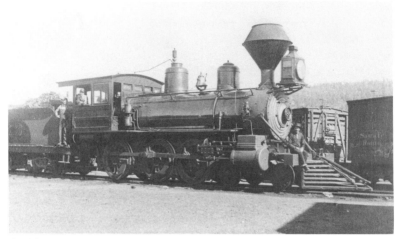

Coal burning Atlantic & Pacific 4-6-0 ten wheeler in the Williams yards. It later became AT&SF 429 class No. 433.   Sullivant Collection

water is in the boiler while going up and down grades is a real skill. While going uphill the water glass is full and downhill it is empty. Somehow, with up to 25 or 30 valves above the boiler head, injectors, fuel preheaters and air flow through the firebox door, temperatures have to be kept up and water levels maintained. Water must be kept above the crown sheet in the boiler or it becomes super-heated. If this happens, water can slosh over the sheet and with the instantaneous burst of steam generated, the boiler will explode. While going uphill with a low water level, the flue tubes can be exposed with the same resulting burst of steam blowing off the front of the locomotive. On an uphill run if there is too much water in the boiler it will flow out of the whistle. Water flowing out of the whistle is no great problem but when too much water is in the boiler it will be forced into the cylinders and it can not be compressed as steam can. Water in the cylinders means a loss of power and must be blown out.

A standing rule exists for low water problems. Stop the locomotive as quickly as possible without sloshing the water. Cut off the fuel flow and get away from the engine until it cools down. Good reasoning!

Firemen lived by the glass and died by the glass. It tells how much water is in the boiler and what to do. Usually the glass is maintained at 1/2 to 3/4 full. The fireman has to be able to read it accurately even with grade changes, power changes and braking. If the glass breaks it is replaced while enroute. A broken water glass in the winter means a cab full of steam-fog and no way to see until the valve is turned off.

172

The weekly local arrives at the Canyon in a snow storm. Crew members prepare to switch No. 830, a 2-8-0 825 class engine onto the wye.

Merrifield-Rinehart Collection, NAU

Fuel is controlled by the fireman as he tries to maintain optimum temperatures. All locomotives, except for the turn-of-the-century days, on the Grand Canyon line have been oil fired. Some required pre-heated oil and others cooler oil. Oil is forced into the firebox under a jet of steam with two valves controlling the flow. One is for the fuel and the other the atomizer. Temperatures are controlled by direct and indirect water lines below the cab that adjust the fuel temperatures before it gets to the firing nozzle. These procedures determine how fine a mixture is sent into the firebox and how far it is thrown forward before burning. Thus the firing rate is adjusted to match the work being done by the engine.

Harassed firemen seldom had any recourse to the occasional hoghead who over-worked and cussed out his fireman for being too slow and always doing the wrong thing. One did have his day though. After a particularly bad run with the Johnson bar in the corner, the throttle wide open and the hoghead constantly on his back about what a rotten job he was doing by not keeping up enough steam, one fireman had had enough. As the train pulled into Williams just about out of water, fuel and steam pressure, the fireman grabbed his bag and slid down the ladder. The hoghead hollered, "Where do you think you're goin'?" To which the fireman replied, "If you're so damn smart about running this engine and firing it too, I'm gonna see how you do it by yourself 'cause I'm goin' home!" And he did!

To become a hoghead requires being a fireman first.

Maybe some of them remembered how hard they worked and the abuse they took on the job from other hogheads. Probably they just passed it on. Others remembered the abuse they received on the way up and treated their firemen with respect and consideration. At any rate, firing is quite a responsible position, particularly on varnish runs. Years of being a fireman and getting to know the equipment and being able to pass the examinations and waiting for an engineer to move or die could make a man a bit coarse around the edges.

Examinations for engineer are quite comprehensive. It has to be this way, particularly on the Grand Canyon line. Nowhere else in the Santa Fe system is an engineer faced with such abrupt changes in grade and curves. Many of the curves are of the ten degree maximum. Horizons are deceiving because it is difficult at times to determine if you are going up hill or down. This line is so demanding that the Santa Fe filmed it for use in a Link simulator designed to train engineers. It has been said that if an engineer can run the Grand Canyon line he can run anywhere on the Santa Fe.

Questions on the examinations covered machinery and air extensively. Everything has to be known about the several brake valves and how to put the steam on one side if necessary to bring in a disabled engine. Rule book questions have to be answered exactly. Santa Fe exams always asked about rule "G." It pertained to the use of liquor and rails commonly paraphrased it: "Thy shalt not haul more than thy tonnage." One question is sort of obvious but usually it got looked at in a funny way. "What is the

1226 class 4-6-2 Pacific No. 1227 ready for a Grand Canyon run at the Williams roundhouse.   Ambrose Collection

first thing you do after leaving the station?" Answer: "Look back to see if the train is following."

Hogheads running steam have their own assortment of valves and levers to control. They can assist the fireman with water problems by using the injectors on the engineer's side (right side) of the cab. Controls are primarily the Johnson bar, throttle, reverse lever and the air for the brakes.

Putting the Johnson bar "in the corner" provides full power. It changes the travel of the valve with respect to the piston except when the reverse lever is on center. In effect, this is the "neutral" position. On center with the reverse lever allows just a slight movement of the valve. Forward or reverse position allows further travel and more steam worked in the cylinder. As speed builds the bar is notched back a bit to keep back pressure from developing. The throttle, through a system of valves, meters the amount of steam from the boiler to the cylinders. As the engineer pulls out on the throttle lever linkage lifts up the throttle valve in the steam dome and steam enters the dry pipe which takes it to the steam chest and then through valves into the cylinders. If the engine is equiped with super heaters the dry pipe takes the steam to the super heater header which sends it through the heater units, back to the header and into the steam chest. When the engineer uses the throttle and Johnson bar properly the steam is used efficiently and provides the most power for the amount of fuel

1337 class 4-6-2 Pacific No. 1370 and 3700 class 4-8-2 Mountain No.3722 wait in front of the El Tovar for the return trip to Los Angeles at the head of "El Tovar" on 15 June 1941.   Ingersoll photo, Bassett Collection

3160 class 2-8-2 Mikado No. 3234 at the engine servicing area just below
Bright Angel Lodge   McCarter Collection

burned.

Air, or the brakes, and its use or misuse has been the subject of many slang terms for engineers. An "air man" is generally considered to be better than average in handling the brakes. Good control of the brakes is imperative. Particularly with the 3800 class locomotives which had notoriously poor brakes. After looking back to see if the train is following, a good hoghead then gets the feel of his train by testing the air. With all of the grades and curves in the next sixty-four miles he has to know when to apply air. For these two and one half hours he is in full cut-off, drifting, braking and half throttle situations.

Speed is a constant consideration. Grades and curves on this line frequently reduce speeds to fifteen and twenty miles per hour. Most steam locomotives didn't have speedometers so the hoghead sat there with watch in hand, counting rail joints, telegraph poles or mileposts to figure his speed with. Later the larger locomotives came equipped with speedometers.

Before the days of two-way radios doubleheaders presented another problem. The engineers in the lead cab and the helper could not communicate. Each had to get a feel for his engine and the other. The lead handled the air—this by regulation. He was also responsible for taking out the slack and getting the train moving. The helper had to know when to add power and slack off. Power was added by the helper after the lead but it had to be eased off prior to the lead. They controlled power to maintain speed and drift as required in order to conserve water and fuel. If they worked together properly a water stop did not have to be made.

Cabs of steam locomotives are noisy, hot and dirty while running. Cinders from the stack of the early coal burners or

3500 class 4-6-2 Pacific No. 3520 leaving the Grand Canyon yard limits with train No. 11.   Merrifield-Rinehart Collection, NAU

from the volcanic ballast always have a way of finding an open eye. Locomotives of the 1600 class rode really rough and the larger 4-8-4s much smoother. Trips to and from the Canyon became a routine of do this here and do that there and watch out for cattle and sheep. Many runs hit something, especially at night. Most times they collided with one or two steers at a time or as many as twenty-some sheep. Sheep are the most dreaded. Wool gets tangled in the running gear and the stomach contents are sprayed up into the cab. It is a real mess to clean up. Worse yet is that sheep can derail a train easier.

But the real obstacle is a large bull. Hitting one of these is an experience unlike any other. Because of the size there is more to be spread all over the cab. One hoghead who was known to be a joker and loved to tell a story had occasion to initiate a new fireman one evening. As the train came up on a bull in the middle of the tracks he told the fireman to put his head outside to make sure the bull cleared the track after being hit. Following orders, the youthful fireman didn't notice the hoghead closing his window. The usual results were obtained with the bull's remains spread all over the cab. Afterwards, the fireman said, "I wore that cow!" He knew better the next time but the hoghead had himself another story to tell on someone.

One might wonder why the hoghead didn't stop the train instead of hitting the livestock. Usually it is too late after seeing the livestock to make a sudden stop without risking injury to passengers. A hoghead trailing varnish has as his first concern the safety of passengers. Better that the railroad pay for dead stock than have injured people.

Hogheads have a tendency to be cantankerous. Maybe it is the years of working hard and taking abuse as a fireman before becoming an engineer or the long hours that make them this way. Whatever it is, there are a lot of good times to help temper their lives and make being a hoghead something to be proud of.

One hoghead in particular was always cantankerous. Early one morning he headed into the Harvey House in Williams for breakfast as usual and he was in no better mood than ever. The Harvey Girl serving customers at the counter was having a bad day also. When he ordered his usual pancakes she returned with the oversized stack on a smaller plate. The hoghead made it plain that he wanted a regular sized plate so he could pour syrup over them. The Harvey Girl, in a round-about earthy way, told him he wasn't going to get another plate. Our hoghead then proceeded to put the cakes on the spotless counter, poured syrup on them and the counter and finished his breakfast. He didn't even leave a tip when he left.

Trains were the focus of life at the Grand Canyon Village for many years. Both the gleaming luxury liners of stainless steel and ordinary coaches of railroad green attracted tourists and villagers alike. But the big attraction of the railroad has always been the pulling power—the locomotives.

There have been at least 33 classes of steam locomotives from the venerable old 4-6-0 and 4-4-0s to the magnificent heavyweights of the 4-8-4 classes that serviced this line from its inception until 1953. Engine number 3893, a 2-10-2 of the 3800 Santa Fe class, probably became the last steam locomotive to make this run in 1953.

It is always interesting to watch a steam locomotive but thrilling comes to mind when consideration is given to the size and power of the larger 4-8-4s and 2-10-2s. Engines of the 3800 class were the largest single group of the 2-10-2s to run the line. Those of the 900, 1600 and 1674 classes had also been used extensively. The 3800s weighed in as the lightest of the heavyweights at a maximum of 710,500 pounds but they had a great tractive force of 75-85,000 pounds. Their ten drivers gave a distinct advantage to these locomotives on the grades of the Canyon line. However, engineers had their hands full running them on the 112 curves of up to 10 degrees radius.

Some of the most impressive locomotives for size, the 3751, 3765 and 3776 classes of the 4-8-4 varitety looked massive.

3700 class 4-8-2 Mountain No. 3748 rests between runs in the engine servicing area at the Grand Canyon.   McCarter Collection

Eastbound Santa Fe Grand Canyon pulled by 3765 class 4-8-4 Northern No. 3775 passes a freight in Cajon Pass.   Santa Fe Railway

3776 class 4-8-4 Northern number 3780 poses for her factory photograph.
Ambrose Collection

3800 class 2-10-2 Santa Fe No. 3859 rests with another 3800 in the engine
servicing area below Bright Angel Lodge.   McCarter Collection

They made up the next-to-heaviest classes ranging from 808,946 to 960,630 pounds. Easy to drive and comfortable to ride, their crews appreciated these hogs over most others. However, with only 65-66,000 pounds of tractive force for all of that weight they were not the most efficient locomotives for this line. They fared much better on the main lines where they could use their speed to advantage.

At 975,400 pounds the 2900 class 4-8-4s certainly became the heaviest class to ply the line. This was the last steam locomotive class purchased by the Santa Fe and saw only limited use on the Canyon line. They appeared nearly identical to the other 4-8-4s and like them the tractive force of the 2900s left something to be desired. They could only produce 66,000 pounds of tractive effort for all of that weight.

Of the two hundred and seventy-six steam locomotives identified to date as having run on the Grand Canyon line, only four are still in existence. Number 2913 is beautifully preserved in a park next to the Mississippi River in Fort Madison, Iowa. Its cousin, 2926, sits quietly in a park in Albuquerque, New Mexico. The state fairgrounds in Topeka, Kansas is the final home of the high-wheel 3463. All of these receive periodic care to preserve and maintain them for public observation. High fences surround these locomotives and keep them distant from those who would otherwise like to personally experience the size and beauty of these mechanical marvels.

The fourth is an exception. Number 3751 is in the process of being restored to operational service by the San Bernardino Railroad Historical Society. Starting in 1986, this non-profit group of dedicated steam devotees rescued 3751 from a park in San Bernardino and has since waged a constant battle for funds to return this class locomotive to the rails she once ranged. Hopefully we will see their success in the form of 3751 recreating the heyday of steam power by heading up a new "El Tovar" passenger special from Los Angeles to the Grand Canyon.

No matter if the equipment is a lightweight or a heavy- weight, there is nothing like steam power and it is at least interesting if not thrilling to watch in operation. And yet its days of ruling the rails were numbered. In February 1938, something new was added to the Grand Canyon scene. On the 10th, diesel unit 822 of the 2 class arrived in a snow storm at the head of the Santa Fe Chief on its maiden voyage from Los Angeles to Chicago. The locomotive sported the livery of the Electro-Motive Corporation as it was their demonstrator and did not belong to the AT&SF.

Hot on its heels on the 18th, diesel unit 6 of the 2 class

Fireman Leo Black and engineer Jim Maule on the pilot of 4000 class 2-8-2 Mikado No. 4095 at the Canyon after a run in the winter of 1948.   Black Collection

San Bernardino Railroad Historical Society crew members removing flues from former AT&SF No. 3751 at California Steel Industries, Fontana, California. This class 4-8-4 Northern engine is one of four steam locomotives still in existence that ran the Grand Canyon line in regular service.
                    SBRHS Photo

made its first appearance at the head of El Capitan. Also arriving in a snow storm, it made a more spectacular contrast to the white snow painted in the new Santa Fe "War Bonnet" livery. On its first Los Angeles to Chicago run, El Capitan made a grand entry to the Canyon. No. 6 was an 1800 horsepower single unit and trailed five stainless steel cars built by Budd Manufacturing Company. This train stayed over on the 19th and left the morning of the 20th.

Neither of these trains were scheduled for the Grand Canyon line. Both came in as extras strictly for the publicity. The Grand Canyon was the plum of the Santa Fe's advertising department and they made the most of it with these two stops. Santa Fe was an innovator with the introduction of diesel power to railroading. Even so, diesels did not become a part of the regular schedule to the Grand Canyon for many a year.

Regularly scheduled diesels first came to the Canyon in 1951. In September, engineer Ray Bartee and fireman Leo Black brought the first unit in as a lead engine. The actual date and the number of the unit have been lost to time. An interesting note is that the day before, they made a test run to see if the diesel could handle the grades of this line. It came in behind a steam locomotive for "insurance."

Steam still ran regularly on the Canyon line even with the introduction of diesels in 1951. Diesels filled out the schedule 100% for the first time in February and March of 1952.

Did the engineers fight the change-over? Not on your life! As one said, "Hogheads fought to get on the diesels. They were a damn sight easier on the eyes, ears and life than those dirty, noisy, stinkin' steam engines." But do they miss the steam? You bet your life they do!

Engineers and Santa Fe management all waited to see how the diesels performed on the three percent grade from Anita to Apex. Steam stalled down at maximum capacity and the diesels did at first also. The underpowered early diesels also had a tendency to burn up the electric traction motors when overloaded. But they proved to be the better engine as power improved. Diesels are less prone to slip down on the slick tracks of the grades during frost or rain because of their lower gear ratio, more uniform distribution of sand and the flexibility of the trucks.

Diesel locomotives only have four to six axle trucks and smaller wheels as compared to the many different size and configurations of trucks and the large drivers of the steam locomotives. This gave them a distinct advantage on the grades and curves of the Grand Canyon line. Steam engines have one to two axle pony trucks in the lead just to guide the longer and heavier

2900 class 4-8-4 Northern No. 2926 rests in a park in Albuquerque, New Mexico. These locomotives weighed in at 975,400 pounds and were the largest to run on the Grand Canyon line. Sister engine No. 2913 rests in a park next to the Mississippi River in Fort Madison, Iowa.

locomotives into the curves. Drivers are larger, not geared and they cover a longer, less flexible distance than the diesels do. Trailing trucks number from none in the smaller engines, to one or two axles in the larger engines just for the purpose of carrying the weight behind the drivers. On this line, one steam locomotive could have as many as sixteen wheels compared to the diesel's eight to twelve.

When the diesels came into regular use the hogheads and firemen faced an unusual problem. The Santa Fe had no training program to teach the crews how to drive them. The hoghead had to learn by watching others and asking questions as he rode in the cab. About every six months, EMC sent an instruction car around to do a show-and-tell on the brake systems. That was about it until in later years the railroad put Link simulators into service. Even the engineer's exam continued to ask a majority of questions on steam for many years after the introduction of diesels. No questions on trouble shooting at all and only a few on the air brakes. Curious procedures for a company that turned out safety brochures and posters by the ton.

As with the steam locomotives, diesels are built for specific jobs but most are utilized for other than their design. They are classed for passenger, freight, passenger/freight and as road switchers. It was not uncommon at a large gathering of extras to see all types represented in the Canyon yards.

Early units came in multiple sets. For instance, the 2 class engines only had the L (lead) unit while 16, 37, 100 and 200 class diesels came in L, A, B and C units. The 300 and 325 classes

First diesel to visit the Grand Canyon, No. 822 sits at the station with the inaugural run of the Santa Fe Chief in 1938. This 2 class engine belonged to EMC and served as their demonstrator.   National Park Service

had L, A and B units and 52 class engines had L and A units. These sets did not remain complete throughout their service either. Units 22A, 24B and 32C could have been coupled with18L. This is why you will not see complete sets in the power roster for diesels.

It is worth noting a couple of unusual types that ran this line. In the 700 class diesels, numbers 726 through 731 used specially built (by Santa Fe) steam generating tenders to provide steam for the passenger cars. They converted six truck tenders and fitted them with a turbine and two boilers each. The Santa Fe painted numbers 9000 through 9004 on the sides in the standard design.

The AT&SF utilized 2650 class diesels of the road switcher variety for several years along the line. Although of the same class individual units differed in that 2651 through 2654 came equipped with a steam generator to handle the passenger cars and others with dynamic brakes. The dynamic brakes were new to the Grand Canyon line at the time these locomotives came on the scene. Dynamic brakes employ an electrical means to convert some of the momentum into heat, thereby providing a retarding force within certain upper and lower speed limits. The two diesels presently operated by the Grand Canyon Railway are of this class but have been completely rebuilt by Santa Fe. The most obvious difference is the high nose of the early versions has been removed for better visibility.

Steam locomotives have been modified and reconfigured for years. Some were simpled (from compound to single cylinders) and others had their wheel arrangement changed to suit them for a new job (main line to switching). Early model diesels also went through rebuildings; older F-7s came out as new road switchers and 1100 class engines went through rebuilding and came out as 3100 class. The major modifications usually resulted in power increases, style and livery changes.

Firemen have gone through the greatest changes with little or nothing for them to do in the eyes of the railroads. Had the railroad companies prevailed, the position of fireman would no longer exist. The "featherbedding" issue was a long and bitter fight between the railroads and the unions and won't be covered here. Suffice to say firemen are still with us and are still a part of the progression to engineer.

When diesels made their appearance on Santa Fe locomotive rosters firemen rejoiced. Among other more comfortable aspects they no longer had to sand flues nor contend with freezing temperatures when the firebox door needed to be opened in the winter for more draft. But firemen found other uncomfortable duties waiting for them in early diesels. Each power unit had two fans and four shutters that had to be adjusted manually. The fireman went outside on the units and made these adjustments as needed. Eventually, even these duties went by the wayside and the firemen became observers and engineer trainees.

Gone also, except for the rare appearance on a scenic line, are the days of doubleheaders and two crews. Now, one engineer handles all of the units from his position in the lead unit.

The second diesel to arrive at the Canyon provided a bit more color. No. 6, also a 2 class engine, sported Santa Fe's new "War Bonnet" livery on the inaugural run of El Capitan.   National Park Service

Communications with other crew members is also handled by radio which is more effective and provides less room for error. The old ways might have been romantic but there are better ways to do things, sometimes.

Steam power is one of those things that lurk in the mind's eye and occupy a favorable memory. No matter that it is "dirty, noisy and stinkin' steam" the mastery of such equipment always evokes pride in a man. If you have pride in your work it is remembered with good feelings. The hoghead doesn't exist who can't find something good to say about steam if he had the opportunity to work with it. The newer breed of diesel engineers also speak well of their equipment and they will remember in years to come of the "good old days." There is good and bad with all things and people have the tendency to remember those things that give them pleasant experiences. Rails have much to be proud of. Rails have good memories.

Like the conductor reading a bill of lading for a sheep stock loader to Quivero asking the hoghead, "What the hell are E-WEs?" The word was "ewes"—female sheep. Good memories.

300 class F-7 number 303 three unit diesel locomotive.   Santa Fe Railway

325 class F-7 No. 338 three unit diesel saw limited service on the Grand Canyon line.   Santa Fe Railway

1200 class GP-30 numbers 1211 and 1214. Engines of this class ran in regular service on the line.   Santa Fe Railway

F-7s and a GP-7 tend to trains stacked up in the yards at the Grand Canyon.   National Park Service

1300 class GP-35 No. 1314 diesel locomotive. GP-35s ran regularly on the Grand Canyon line in the 1950s and 60s.   Santa Fe Railway

Boy Scout specials jam the Grand Canyon yards in 1953. 2650 class GP-7s, 200 and 300 class F-7s head up the specials.   National Park Service

MOTIVE POWER ROSTER FOR THE GRAND CANYON RAILWAY

This roster of steam and diesel locomotives that plied the Grand Canyon line until the last trains in 1974 has been compiled from photographs, accident reports, train sheets, train orders, log books, telegrams, newspaper articles and personal interviews.

STEAM [All manufactured by Baldwin unless otherwise noted]

Class	Type	Number
	4-8-0	SFP 19 (Rhode Island)
	4-6-0	SFP 49, 51
	4-6-0	SFP 70 (Pittsburgh)
	4-4-0	SFP 88 (New York)
23	4-4-0	33 (Schenectady)
41	4-4-0	45, 49 (Schenectady)
125	4-4-0	125 (New York)
281	4-6-0	281, 282
354	4-6-0	370 (Pittsburgh)
468	4-6-0	470, 475, 485, 486, 495 (Rhode Island)
566	2-6-0	610
631	4-8-0	637 (Rhode Island)
649	2-8-0	649
664	2-8-0	678
709	2-8-0	722 (Dickson)

769	2-8-0	782 (Richmond)
789	2-8-0	791, 795, 806, 809, 811, 812
825	2-8-0	830, 833, 836, 840
900	2-10-2	907, 909, 911, 923, 942, 947, 948, 953, 954, 955, 956, 958, 959, 960, 963, 964, 965, 968, 976, 978, 979, 984
1226	4-6-2	1227, 1229, 1230, 1235, 1239, 1241, 1242, 1251, 1252, 1256, 1258
1270	4-6-2	1272
1309	4-6-2	1309, 1322, 1331, 1332, 1333, 1334
1337	4-6-2	1337, 1338, 1339, 1340, 1341, 1342, 1343, 1364, 1367, 1368, 1369, 1370, 1371, 1372, 1373, 1376, 1378, 1379
1600	2-10-2	1620, 1623, 1624, 1627, 1628, 1629, 1630, 1632, 1633, 1634, 1638, 1640, 1653, 1659, 1663, 1665, 1669, 1672, 1673
1674	2-10-2	1675, 1676, 1677, 1680, 1681, 1682, 1683, 1684, 1685, 1687, 1689, 1690, 1691, 1692
1800	2-6-2	1800, 1812, 1816, 1823, 1827, 1833, 1839, 1844, 1850, 1859, 1886
1950	2-8-0	1959, 1960, 1961, 1963, 1965, 1966, 1967, 1968, 1970, 1971, 1972, 1985, 1990
2160	4-6-0	2173
2900	4-8-4	2913, 2917, 2926
3100	2-8-2	3119
3129	2-8-2	3136, 3139, 3142, 3143, 3151, 3152, 3153, 3154, 3155
3160	2-8-2	3210, 3229, 3230, 3234, 3238, 3240, 3241, 3243, 3254, 3256
3450	4-6-4	3456
3460	4-6-4	3463, 3465
3500	4-6-2	3520, 3521, 3522, 3524, 3525, 3526, 3529, 3531, 3532, 3534
3700	4-8-2	3701, 3703, 3704, 3705, 3706, 3707, 3708, 3710, 3711, 3721, 3722, 3726, 3727, 3728, 3731, 3734, 3735, 3736, 3737, 3738, 3739, 3740, 3741, 3742, 3743, 3744, 3745, 3746, 3747, 3748, 3749, 3750
3751	4-8-4	3751, 3753, 3754, 3755, 3756, 3758, 3760, 3761, 3763, 3764
3765	4-8-4	3767, 3768, 3770, 3771, 3772, 3774
3776	4-8-4	3777, 3780, 3781, 3784, 3785
3800	2-10-2	3807, 3818, 3833, 3837, 3939, 3850, 3851, 3852, 3853, 3854, 3855, 3856, 3857, 3858, 3859, 3860, 3861, 3862, 3863, 3864, 3865, 3866, 3867, 3876,

3877, 3878, 3879, 3880, 3881, 3882, 3884, 3885,
3887, 3888, 3891, 3892, 3893, 3894, 3895, 3897,
3898, 3899, 3900, 3901, 3902, 3903, 3904, 3905,
3906, 3907, 3909, 3910, 3911, 3912, 3913, 3914,
3915, 3925, 3927, 3931, 3932, 3933, 3934, 3935,
3936, 3937, 3938, 3939, 3940

4000   2-8-2   4005, 4007, 4010, 4013, 4014, 4033, 4036, 4059

Possible other classes utilized: 507, 1290, 1452 and 5000.

DIESEL [All manufactured by EMD* unless otherwise noted]

Class	Model	Type	Number
2	E-2	A1A-A1A	6, 822 (EMC*)
16	F-3	B-B	16L, 17L, 18A, 18L, 19L, 22A, 22C, 22L, 24A, 27C, 28L, 30A, 30B, 31A, 32A, 32B, 32C, 33L, 34A, 35L
37	F-7	B-B	37A, 38A, 38L, 39C, 41L, 42A, 44A, 44L, 45C
52	PA-2	A1A-A1A	54A, 57L, 76L (AlCo*)
100	FTA/B	B-B	155, 415
200	F-7	B-B	250L, 254L, 257L, 259L, 263L, 273L
300	F-7	B-B	302L, 307L, 310L, 312A, 312B, 313B, 313L, 314A
325	F-7	B-B	325L, 328L, 328A, 329L, 329A, 334A, 340L, 363L (this last unit is a guess as to class as it does not appear in the record); these became Amtrak power.
700	GP-9	B-B	717, 726, 727, 728, 729, 730, 731, 735, 744, 747 (726-731 used steam generating tenders 9000-9004)
1200	GP-30	B-B	1201, 1208, 1210, 1216, 1221, 1223, 1225, 1226, 1232, 1234, 1235, 1241, 1243, 1244, 1246, 1248, 1251, 1254, 1257, 1260, 1262, 1263, 1264, 1266, 1267, 1269, 1270, 1274, 1277, 1278, 1279, 1280, 1282
1300	GP-35	B-B	1300, 1302, 1303, 1304, 1305, 1315, 1317, 1333, 1334, 1337, 1338, 1339, 1340, 1342, 1346, 1348, 1350, 1352, 1357, 1359, 1367, 1369, 1370, 1373, 1377, 1378, 1385, 1387, 1388, 1390, 1391, 1394, 1395, 1401, 1404, 1405, 1408, 1409, 1410, 1413, 1418, 1419,

192

			1420, 1425, 1437, 1439, 1440, 1456
2650	GP-7	B-B	2651, 2653, 2654, 2659, 2692
3100	GP-20	B-B	3151
3200	GP-30	B-B	3210, 3211, 3212, 3236, 3238, 3239, 3241, 3244, 3245, 3250, 3251, 3254, 3269, 3270, 3274, 3280, 3282
3300	GP-35	B-B	3309, 3317, 3337, 3340, 3342, 3349, 3352, 3370, 3372, 3388, 3390, 3397, 3402, 3409, 3410, 3411, 3416, 3424, 3432, 3439, 3441, 3442, 3444, 3447, 3448, 3451, 3453, 3460

*EMD — Electro-Motive Division of General Motors Corporation
*EMC — Electro-Motive Corporation
*ALCo — American Locomotive Company

MOTIVE POWER ROSTER, 1989-1999
Grand Canyon Railway Steam

Class	Type	Number
SC-3	2-8-0	29 (Former LS&I)
SC-4	2-8-0	18, 19, 20 (Former LS&I)
0-1A	2-8-2	4960 (Former CB&Q)

Grand Canyon Railway Diesel

Model	Type	Number
GP-7	B-B	2072, 2134 (Former AT&SF)
FPA-4	B-B	6762, 6773, 6776, 6788, 6793 (Former CN)
FPB-4	B-B	6860, 6871 (Former CN)

Foreign Diesel

Line	Model	Type	Number
A&C	GP-9	B-B	3802
Amtrak	P-32BWH	B-B	503, 505, 507, 508, 509, 512, 514
	F-40PH	B-B	217, 291, 305, 315, 334, 358, 364, 369, 373, 393, 406
	P40B	B-B	815, 816, 818, 822, 823, 830
	P42B	B-B	1, 7, 20, 25, 30, 31, 36, 45, 46, 48, 68, 72, 74, 80, 88
AT&SF	FP-45	C-C	100, 101 (Now BNSF 90, 91)
	GP-30	B-B	2713, 2728, 2769
	8-40BW	B-B	520, 559
	SD40-2	C-C	5111
	SDF40-2	C-C	5259
BNSF	9-44CW	C-C	1039
Siemens	Sprinter	B-B	RS1
WS	E-9A	A1A-A1A	10A, 10C

MUST ALL GOOD THINGS COME TO AN END?

"All good things must come to an end." Most of us have heard something similar to this phrase over the years. Apparently that saying does not apply to the Grand Canyon Railway. There have been times, particularly in 1942 and 1968, when people actually believed this line had come to its natural end. Even through the 1970s and '80s most believed this railroad would never again carry passengers. On the 17th of September, 1989, that all changed.

Nothing remains exactly the same as when it began. Everything changes and that is the natural order. Historically, our railroad has followed this rule from the date of conception in the minds of the men who brought her into being. The Santa Fe and Grand Canyon Railroad became The Grand Canyon Railway followed by the Grand Canyon Branch of the Atchison, Topeka and Santa Fe Railway and then partially owned by Railroad Resources, Inc. The rule is still being applied as the railroad is now owned and operated by a new company called the Grand Canyon Railway. After an infusion of fifteen million dollars and a lot of hard work the company began operations on the eighty-eighth anniversary of the original passenger run to the Canyon.

Grand Canyon National Park draws travelers from all countries. Visitors always consider their means of transportation to and from the Canyon. Historically railroads have been developers in this country and although natural forces built the Grand Canyon the Santa Fe developed and built most of the

Class engine No. 1800, a 2-6-2 Prairie waits at Grand Canyon station with the crew and station personnel for the last regularly scheduled Williams-Grand Canyon passenger run of World War II.   Kolb photo, NAU Special Collections

facilities for tourists. The United States government subsidized highway and airline travel in the form of federal highways, airports and aids-to-navigation but had nothing for the railroads. Their operations still had to come out of the corporate pocket book. In short, the government funded the railroad's competition.

In the mid 1920s, the roads to the Park had not progressed beyond dirt and gravel. Actually two roads serviced the "south entrance." One originated at Flagstaff and the other at Maine (more commonly called Parks today). The Park Service continually requested a paved road, the federal subsidies to do the work, and entreated Senator Carl Hayden to visit the Park in order to determine the necessity for such a project.

The canny Park Service administrators invited him to visit during the "Monsoon" season knowing if Hayden saw the roads to be in terrible shape they would get the money. During this time of the year heavy thunderstorms made the Maine road a quagmire. This is the route the Senatorial party traveled with Park Service personnel as guides. It didn't take them long to get stuck axle deep in the mud. Several tows by handy teams of horses got them free and on their way. The Park got one hundred thousand dollars the next year for a paved road from Williams to the Grand Canyon.

This highway subsidy was the beginning of the end for Santa Fe passenger service to the Canyon. As automobile and airplane travel increased, so decreased the numbers of rail passengers. As passenger revenues decreased, so did profits for the Santa Fe stockholders. The Grand Canyon line had become a liability. Her days were numbered.

But it had not always been so. If any time can be called the "golden days" of the Grand Canyon Railway, the 1920s have to be given serious consideration for the lead. Although no year ever saw 100,000 passengers cross the rails to the Grand Canyon, 1927 came the closest with 70,382. Even in 1953, when the Boy Scouts of America took the Canyon by storm with 20,000 passengers in an eight day period, the total only reached 54,919.

If one considers only the revenue passenger totals 1927 had been a "golden year" indeed. But maybe not! For it is also on record as the first year the number of automobile passengers entering the Park exceeded the number of rail passengers. The totals didn't even come close because the autos brought 7,048 more people in than did the trains. This couldn't be right! Railroads had been around for nearly a century and in reality, automobiles for less than a third of that. To make matters worse, buses began regular scheduled delivery of passengers to the gates of the Park the following year. They brought 224 people in 1928.

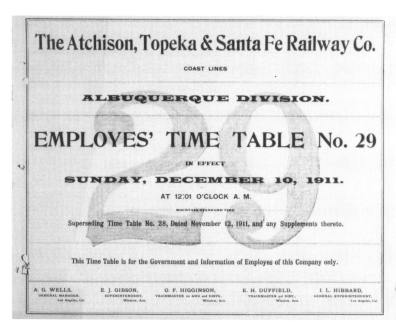

AT&SF Coast Lines time table for the Albuquerque Division which included the Grand Canyon line dated 10 December 1911.

The Grand Canyon Railway Company time table which was a part of the AT&SF table No. 29 from the same date.

Automobiles gave people the freedom of choice. While traveling on federally built highways, people can stop whenever or wherever it pleases them. Railroads run on a schedule. To ride a train, as pleasurable as it may be, one is required to travel at the convenience of the railroad and stop only at scheduled stations. This combination of roads paid for by the government and freedom of choice offered by the automobile proved to be more than railroad passenger service could cope. Interestingly, this circumstance is in the process of a reversal with the new Grand Canyon Railway. Motor vehicles now choke the Park's roads and many motorists are finding it more relaxing to ride the train.

Buses also proved more convenient to out-of-the-way towns and cities not serviced by railroads. As highways became more and more extensive, this enabled buses to pick off many previously loyal railroad customers. Small tour groups are more easily arranged for with buses. Special cars and trains are expensive and required larger numbers of people in a group to make reservations. Buses can pull up to the front door and load on forty people or so and deliver them to their destination's front door.

When airplanes first arrived at the Grand Canyon in 1933 with 107 passengers, another trend began that further eroded railroad passenger service on the Grand Canyon line. Even

GCRy Company time table No. 48 showing changes in train numbers and flag stops.

then a network of LF (low frequency) aids-to-navigation existed — all paid for by the government. Many years passed before air traffic to the Canyon resulted in a large number of visitors. Even by 1966 the total only reached 9,842 for the year.

But the precedent had been set. Federally funded projects for alternate means of transportation began the death knell for American railroad passenger travel. Federal subsidies for railroads did not come about until many had gone under or had reduced both passenger and freight service drastically. By then it was too late. Today's Amtrak, with its greatly reduced mileage and heavy subsidies, can barely compete. And now, although in better condition than in years past, Amtrak totters on the brink of extinction. The Grand Canyon Branch of the AT&SFRy did not survive the corporate-federal crunch.

Railway passenger service to the Canyon declined drastically in the two years preceeding the beginning of the Great Depression. When the Depression hit late in 1929, revenue passenger totals dropped by more than 16,000 from the high in 1927. The skid continued until they hit rock bottom in 1933 with a total of 11,239 people transiting the line from Williams to the Grand Canyon.

Confirmation of the trouble yet to come is shown in the statistics for automobile passengers entering the park. More people came in automobiles this worst year of the railroad to date, than came by railroad in the best year of 1927. In 1933 73,034 auto passengers checked in through the entrances to the Park.

Buses didn't fare much better, but they did manage an increase in business. In this dismal year of 1933 4,614 bus passengers came to see the wonders of the Canyon. Remember too, this was the inaugural year of scheduled air service with their 107 first-of-a-kind passengers.

By 1932 Santa Fe management saw the handwriting on the wall. At the end of 1931 only 34,549 revenue passengers rode the train to the Canyon. Two scheduled trains made the daily trip in each direction and after the March 1932 schedule came out in print only one first class passenger train appeared on the schedule for the daily round trip. This cancelled train became the first casualty of the passenger crunch.

Up until the schedule came out in March of 1932, there had been few changes in the trains except for times of arrivals and departures. In 1901 the schedule listed two trains; northbound No. 10 and southbound No. 11. An increase in traffic by 1905 dictated the addition of two trains; No. 14 northbound and No. 15 southbound. For some reason in 1910 these numbers

Grand Canyon Railway staff in front of the Grand Canyon depot at the 10 January 1989 announcement for the rebuilding of the line. (l. to r.) Lois Klein, public relations; Bob Roth, president; Thelma Biegert, secretary-treasurer; Max Biegert, chairman; Brian Alexander, vice president; Al Richmond, historian.

changed to 12 and 14 northbound and 11 and 15 southbound. And so it remained until the 1932 schedule change of one train in each direction with No. 14 becoming the southbound and No. 15 becoming the northbound. This last train numbering endured until 30 July 1968 with only the World War II hiatus causing a temporary change.

With resumption of service after the War on 30 May 1946, the lull from 1942 had caused the printed schedules to show a blank space for the Grand Canyon District. The schedule of June 1946 corrected this and from that date until the September 1946 schedule appeared the northbound train is listed as 124 and the southbound as 123. The September schedule returned the numbers of 14 and 15 to their original directions.

Over a period of years several Santa Fe trains used numbers 123 and 124 but while in Grand Canyon service they became the "El Tovar." Originally they appeared as a summer supplementary train from Kansas City to Los Angeles via the Grand Canyon in 1940. Management revised the schedule in 1941 with round trip service between Los Angeles and Grand Canyon. Military personnel on recuperative leave made up a majority of the passengers during the war. El Tovar also picked up and dropped off cars at Williams for through service on other trains, usually

Vintage 1923 Pullman built Harriman style car being lifted onto a flat bed for transportation from Oakland to Richmond, California for rebuilding of the trucks in January, 1989.

trains 23 and 24. Consists as published in the June to September 1946 schedule included a sufficient number of the following cars: dormitory lounge, sleeping, tourist sleeper, dining and chair. El Tovar disappeared forever from the schedules in 1946 and trains 123 & 124 with it until April of 1950 when they reappeared as the Grand Canyon Limited (the name trains 23 and 24 ran under).

During the war years break from scheduled passenger service, the weekly local made regular Tuesday runs (mostly freight) under the numbers of 231 for the northbound and 232 for the southbound. Only the change from Tuesday operations to Wednesdays for switching convenience in the yards on 1 June 1959 is in the record.

All of these number changes had nothing to do with the operation of specials. Special trains, in as many sections as necessary, continued to visit the Canyon over the years. Even after the discontinuation of scheduled passenger service in 1968, specials continued to make their way in and out of the Grand Canyon Village along with the weekly local.

On 17 September 1951, the Grand Canyon line celebrated it's golden anniversary. Fifty years prior, the first scheduled passenger train made its way from Williams to the south rim of the Grand Canyon. By 1951 problems with dwindling passenger revenues had become acute. Santa Fe records show only 34,377

201

paying passengers for the year. The previous year, 1950, had done considerably better with 48,097. By 1954, revenues stabilized at about 35,000 per year. As most of these passengers traveled in the summer months of June through September something had to give.

The first of November, 1955 saw the first drastic change in the service offered by the railroad to the rim. On this day, Fred Harvey buses began the transfer of Santa Fe passengers from Williams to the Canyon during the months of November through May 1956. From 1956 until 1968, the scheduled buses ran from 30 September to 25 May. This served as continuation of Santa Fe railroad service with the passengers being ticketed from their point of origin through to the Canyon. The buses merely operated under a lease agreement. Remember if you will, the Fred Harvey Company had bought out the Santa Fe interests at the Canyon the previous year except for the depot and yards. As this constituted railroad service the Grand Canyon station remained the destination of the buses.

Curtailment of off season train service helped somewhat but the losses continued to mount. By 1960 passenger revenues dropped below the 10,000 mark and by 1967 had gone off the charts to 4,658. Decision time for the board members of the Atchison, Topeka and Santa Fe Railway Company arrived in 1966. Even with the off season reduction in service, passenger revenues at the 6,000 level could not justify the continuation of scheduled service to the Canyon. When 1967 rolled around, they decided to shut down the railroad.

Considering some of the figures the Santa Fe people worked with at this time, one gets the idea rather quickly as to the need for discontinuation. For this time period, they considered 1961 a typical year for service along the Grand Canyon Branch. The following carloads were recorded to or from the indicated stations:

Cargo	Red Lake	Grand Canyon	Willaha	Anita
Sheep & goats	17	3	16	
Cattle		9	20	
Feed		2		
Sand & gravel		105		
Autos		2		
Oil & gas		150		
Water		300	1	3
Petroleum products	3			
Machinery	1			

Williams depot and Fray Marcos Hotel in 1984. The ballast regulator to the right had been run over the line in the preliminary survey done by Railroad Resources.

The Fray Marcos on 29 March 1989, the day restoration began. Note the advanced state of deterioration.

Couple this meager traffic with 9,090 revenue passengers and the picture is indeed bleak. Add figures in succeeding years of $6,730 in Pullman operations losses in 1965 and $7,622 in 1966, tack on figures for 1967 of a freight high of 22,444 tons in December and a low of 7,123 tons in August, then consider a passenger high of 2,200 in August and a low of 13 in March and there is no other conclusion. The Grand Canyon Branch would barely make its diamond anniversary and never see its 75th!

While the Santa Fe management considered these problems, a major east-west track realignment got underway. In 1960 and 1961, the company began and completed construction of a new double track north of the main line. Years of problems on the troublesome curves, grades and tunnel of the existing main line through Johnson Canyon made this bypass a necessity. The new main line allows greater speed and safety of operation. Along with the realignment came a new station.

When the new track went into service on 19 December 1961 Williams' Agent Glenn Irvin moved his office from the old Williams Depot and opened the doors of the new depot shown on the timetable as Williams Junction. Now, the Grand Canyon trains bypassed Williams and added three miles each way to the

Grand Canyon Railway GP-7s on company tracks under their own power for the first time on 26 April 1989. (l. to r.) Bob Roth, president; Max Biegert, chairman; John James, roadmaster; Al Richmond, historian; Gary Bensman, chief mechanical officer; Brian Alexander, vice president and Will Ambrose, engineering consultant.

run. The new station was east of Williams and the Canyon trains used the same north-south tracks plus part of the old main line on their new route. This pleasant looking new station's days were numbered from the day it opened its doors.

When train No. 14 rolled into Williams Junction, to end the tourist season on 23 September 1967, the Santa Fe planned to make this the last scheduled passenger run of the Grand Canyon line. On 25 April 1968, the Atchison, Topeka and Santa Fe Railway Company notified the Arizona Corporation Commission by letter they had no intentions of continuing service from Williams Junction to the Grand Canyon in 1968 with lost revenues listed as their justification.

However, it did not end here. The Corporation Commission held a hearing at the Canyon in May and returned a finding that service was "reasonably necessary." A Commission order on 26 May directed the railroad to resume service and continue through 5 September. Still, it did not end here. Santa Fe did in fact resume operations but tackled the problem in the Arizona Supreme Court. The court reversed the decision of the Arizona Corporation Commission and on 24 July 1968, ordered discontinuation of passenger service.

Without Emery Kolb to record the scene for posterity as he did the "last train" in 1942, and without press coverage or even a fond farewell from a crowd of railroad personnel, train No.

Surfacing machine works on the depot track one week before opening. Note new windows in same design as when first installed, refinished exterior of the Fray Marcos and the original 1908 brick platform.

205

14 pulled out of the Grand Canyon for Williams Junction at 5:30 PM on 30 July 1968. A consist of diesel engine No. 730 with one baggage car and one coach certainly did not make for a grand last train. Yet, in its limited capacity, it represented almost sixty-seven years of passenger service history that has little parallel within this country's railroads.

Maybe Engineer V. J. Conway thought of this as he gave the horn two short blasts and moved the throttle back to begin the last trip. Fireman J. E. Bland might have noticed the powerhouse and the laundry slide by with a bit of regret. It has gone unrecorded if any passengers rode on this last train but one might assume at least a few did. As conductor J. D. Hart checked their tickets while the train gathered speed and moved out of the yards he must have considered this was to be the last time for him to be taking care of these duties on this run. Grand Canyon Agent D. L. Burns thought about it for he kept the original copy of the message terminating service and the clearance card. Conversation must have been at a minimum. What can one say when a way of life comes to an end?

The end occurred at Williams Junction with this notation on the Dispatcher's train sheet: "No. 14 and 15 discontinued on arrival Williams Jct July 30, 1968" with the time probably about the scheduled arrival of 7:15 PM. No one came to say anything for nothing more could be said. That statement on the train sheet laid the Grand Canyon Railway to rest.

Specials, cattle extras, work extras, weekly freights and ore shipments continued along the line for a few years on a helter-skelter, as-needed basis. Ore shipments stopped in 1969

Newly resurfaced tangent track south of Red Lake station just a few days before the running of the re-inaugural train on 17 September.

and cattle extras made their last appearance in 1973. Regular freights and all service to Grand Canyon stopped with the closure of the Grand Canyon Depot in 1969.

Early in 1969 when the AT&SF applied again to the Arizona Corporation Commission to suspend all services to the Canyon no argument or court action ensued. Permission was granted. On 13 May, a company message directed the closure of the Grand Canyon Depot at the end of shift on 16 May 1969. Agent Burns did so, but remained until 20 May to close out the railroad's business. A subsequent message closed the depot at Williams Junction on 2 June 1969. For Agent Irvin this routine brought no pleasure as he had closed the Williams Depot and disposed of its property eight years previously. These actions sealed both ends of a once vital railroad.

The roadmaster added a small footnote to train traffic on the line. In the summer of 1974 he decided to recover the usable track and materials along the right-of-way. The dispatcher at Winslow sent two work extras in June for this purpose. On 13 June, engines 3372 and 3441 with Conductor P. D. Kirkland and Engineer R. G. Long at the controls, took the section gang and a string of gondolas to the Canyon in order to retire rail and fastenings. Then on 20 June, Conductor W. S. Peterson and Engineer E. Sanchez made the trip north with engines 3402 and 3388 for the loaded material. As he notched the throttle back, Engineer Sanchez had no idea he was operating the last Atchison,

Number 19 in livery of Lake Superior and Ishpeming Railroad. Built in 1910 for this road by Alco, she served on this line until 1960. The GCRy plans to overhaul No. 19 for service in 1991.

Topeka and Santa Fe Railway train out of Grand Canyon for the next sixteen years. He did his job that sunny Thursday and as far as he knew, there would probably be another train some day.

For many people a way of life came to an end on that day in 1974. No more passengers. No more ore trains. No more cattle extras. No more log trains. No more water trains. No more grand specials. People in Williams, along the line and at the Grand Canyon became used to a life without the railroad. Most believed the trains would never run again. In spite of these feelings some day has come for now we have a revitalized Grand Canyon Railway. But it did not come quick or easy.

If a railroad ever had a personality it is the Grand Canyon line. Something like this cultural system should not be allowed to die. Several individuals tried to revive it as a tourist attraction in the late 1970s and early 1980s. All failed because they had no personal investment at stake in the project. These situations of "I will run a railroad and make a fortune for myself if you will give me the money" just did not have a chance. Some solicited funds from the federal government and sources other than their own. No personal interest—no go!

Then in 1980, the AT&SFRy filed for abandonment and salvage of the Grand Canyon District with the Arizona Corporation Commission. After all of the legal dust settled, the ACC granted the request and the Santa Fe contracted with a railroad salvage company to do the work.

Enter Railroad Resources, Inc. of Phoenix, Arizona. This company, which specialized in leasing or sales of used rolling stock, salvage of railroad materials, dismantling of railroad properties and railroad construction, took another look at the Grand Canyon line. President Charles Newman and vice-president Brian Alexander saw the potential for a revival of this line in the form of a vintage railroad as a tourist attraction.

When they contracted with the Santa Fe for the dismantling of the line in 1983, they had already looked at the road for one of the previous promoters. After completing several feasibility studies, checking the bank balance and borrowing additional funds, Railroad Resources purchased the right-of-way, with options on the Fray Marcos Hotel and depot in Williams and other adjacent properties from the Santa Fe for the grand sum of $4,295,128.00 on 30 May 1984. This purchase of the right-of-way and properties in Williams comprised one hundred four parcels of land for a total of 1,780.7 acres.

In March 1984, Railroad Resources ran a ballast regulator over the line from Williams to a point just outside of the

Two Grand Canyon Railway tenders and No. 20 pass by Flagstaff's station on 27 August 1989 enroute to Williams. The loads required 100 ton flat cars. Avery photo

Park boundary. After clearing the weeds, brush and small trees from the tracks they made an assessment of the costs required to put the line back into operation. The rails remained in good shape but many bolts needed replacement because the expansion and contraction from the heat and cold had sheared them off. An estimated 20,000 ties needed to be replaced before operations could commence and a couple of small washouts and several bridge abutments needed to be overhauled. Virtually all of the roadbed along the right-of-way and in the Grand Canyon yards needed reballasting. All of this work required several months.

The company stockpiled ties and spotted ballast cars in the yards at Williams. Brian Alexander identified for purchase fourteen clerestory (sometimes called clearstory) roof, 86 seat coaches built by the Standard Steel Car Company belonging to the New Jersey Transit Authority and ten Pullman built Harriman style 96 seat coaches owned by the Southern Pacific and stored in Oakland, California. He conducted searches for motive power and gave consideration to several possibilities.

The people of Williams began to gear up for a railroad. This looked like a serious venture and after the false starts of previous promotors people dared to hope again. Many doubters expressed their opinions but grudgingly some of them started to come around. In the end the doubter's cries of "I told you so" hurt the most. The president of Railroad Resources refused to relinquish the controlling interest of the company in return for investment capital. Under these circumstances potential investers refused to back the project. Railroad Resources folded and with it went the plans for the Grand Canyon Line.

But the people of Williams were not ready to give up on the railroad as yet. This project meant too much to the economy of the city. Ever since the Santa Fe stopped passenger service to the Canyon and the railroad by-passed the city in the early sixties, the town's economy rode a downward spiral. In 1986 the highway department completed the last link in Interstate 40 and it effectively killed Route 66 through the city. These two actions virtually sealed the town off from the traveling public. Several civic leaders continually worked hard to keep Williams from becoming a ghost town.

To them the railroad was a vital component for rehabilitation of the city's dying economy. They fought every attempt to scrap the line for the steel and ties. When men and machinery arrived to salvage the tracks in town, as in a scene out of the Old West the City Marshall arrested the contractor for not having a permit and confiscated the equipment. This delayed them for a while but they moved out of the town limits and ripped up one mile of ties from milepost five to six.

Fortunately, in the search for funds a loan had been made to Railroad Resources by businessman Max Biegert. Foreclosure on the note gave him title to the upper twenty miles of track. After clearing the field of would-be pretenders at a City

Looking forlorn and stripped, No. 18 awaits unloading in Williams on 20 August 1989.

Council sponsored public meeting, Mr. Biegert determined the feasibility of the project, purchased the remainder of the track and property and began to run a railroad.

Max and his wife, Thelma, came up the hard way after his service in World War Two. He scraped together all of the cash he could and began a crop dusting business with one war surplus Stearman and a lot of grit. They did well in a world wide aerial application business known as Biegert Aviation International and another company, National Child Care. After finding themselves in the railroad business they attempted to arrange additional financing for the project. But, because of all the previous problems created by promotors the banks refused to consider their proposition. Max and Thelma then reached deep into their pockets, tapped other resources available to them and came up with the fifteen million dollars necessary to get the first train to the Canyon.

Assembly of a first class team to make the project work became the next priority. Max took the reins as Chairman and Chief Executive Officer. Thelma, with the experience earned in their businesses over the years, assumed the position of Secretary-Treasurer. Robert Roth came on board as President and Chief Operating Officer with many years of recreational business acumen gained in the trenches of such companies as Holiday Inn and Del Webb. Brian Alexander's extensive civil engineering and railroad experience made his selection as Vice President Railroad

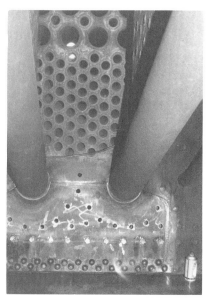

Boiler patch in No. 18 is typical of the high quality work accomplished by the Mechanical Department in preparation for running on 17 September.

Operations and Construction a natural choice. These four principals formed the nucleus of the team.

All through 1988, the officers and consultants completed feasibility studies, planned, located and purchased equipment, hired key personnel and formulated a plan of action. On 10 January 1989, at the historic Grand Canyon depot, the company principals announced the plan to the world with a major press conference. "The Grand Canyon Railway is for real. Operations will begin with a steam train from Williams to the Grand Canyon on 17 September 1989, the eighty-eighth anniversary of the first passenger train in 1901." The media gave the project good coverage across the country. Skeptics abounded but in short order their tune changed as they observed the company's progress.

Work began on the tracks, engines, cars and the renovation of the Fray Marcos Hotel and depot in Williams with the company goal to run the reinaugural train and open the facilities to the public on the 17th. Scheduled for use as the southern terminus of the line, the Fray Marcos would return from status as a derelict building to one of prominence within the City of Williams. Already on the National Register for Historic Places as the largest and oldest poured concrete building in Arizona, the Fray Marcos is the southern anchor of this historic railroad.

The principals outlined future plans which call for a spur line to the Grand Canyon airport at Tusayan, two hotels, an Old West theme park and maintenance facilities. No small project this, it is estimated to take eighty million dollars and up to eight years for completion. Management agreed early on to make this a truly first class historical project. To this end, they included in the plans a museum open to the public free of charge and will use vintage equipment whenever possible.

It is difficult to imagine a more hectic nine months than the period from January to September, 1989. The company literally had to begin with nothing more than a derelict building, sixty-five miles of weather-beaten track and a nucleus of people. Within nine short months everything had to come together. To accomplish these seemingly impossible tasks, Max and his team built an even larger team of experts.

Roadmaster John James hired on and assumed responsibility for rebuilding the right-of-way. To do so required the locating and purchasing of 30,000 ties, finding track equipment and hiring the best available men to do the work. James used his years of railroad construction experience and contacts to locate people of the highest qualifications. Retired Santa Fe Division Engineer "Tex" Garland reported in as the maintenance-of-way consultant. He had been responsible for the Grand Canyon line

Thelma and Max Biegert on the pilot of No. 29 the day it arrived in Williams. No. 29 will be in service for the 1990 season.

during his employment with the Santa Fe. Retired Santa Fe Bridge & Building foreman Cliff Gipson (with fifty four years of railroad experience) served as GCRy railroad bridges and structures consultant. Sam Imbleau and John Morris headed up the track gangs. These men and the gangs worked long, hard days through the spring and summer in order to make the deadline.

Work began at milepost five on 29 March with the replacement of one mile of ties stolen from the roadbed. Track gangs and bridge & building crews coordinated their schedules and began the sixty-five mile march to the south rim. In a little over five months the track gangs walked this distance at least several times in the course of their work and the B&B crew visited every bridge and culvert. They pulled and replaced ties, rails, beams and spikes by the thousands. As they completed the basic work ballast trains followed up on the crews and replaced the volcanic cinders which had been depleted by years of erosion. Ballast regulators and surfacing machines then made the final adjustments by tamping ballast, leveling and straightening the tracks and finishing the surface. On the first of August the crews reached the yards at the Grand Canyon and on the fourteenth of September they presented Max Biegert with a 24 carat gold spike maul and the Grand Canyon Railway with a first class right-of-way.

Chief Mechanical Officer Gary Bensman faced a task which on the surface defied common sense. Where, in 1989, are to

Under a lowering sky and a cloud of red, white and blue balloons, No. 18 pulls out of the Williams station at 12:00 noon on 17 September for the re-inaugural run to the Grand Canyon with honorary engineer Will Ambrose at the controls.

No. 18 at the Grand Canyon on 17 September 1989 rests under the shadow of the El Tovar Hotel while crowds gather around for a look at the first steam engine to enter the yards since 1953.

Newsboys pass out copies of the *Territorial Times* on the day of the re-inaugural run. The headline tells the story.

be found the vintage locomotives and qualified steam personnel needed to run this line? The enginemen (and woman) turned out to be the least difficult. Gary, with his extensive background in the twilight world of American steam scenic railroads, knew most of these people at least by reputation. They came from as far as Georgia in the person of master mechanic Robert Franzen. Enginemen came from all over; Phil Eskew, Arizona; Ervin White, Connecticut; Mike Ramsey, Colorado; Kent McClure, Illinois; Russ and Marty Fischer, New Mexico; and Robert Crossman & Charles Harris, Texas. Retired Santa Fe engineer Will Ambrose, with over thirty years experience with steam and diesel, served as GCRy locomotive consultant. His experience includes design engineering with the Baldwin Locomotive Works and service as a locomotive engineer on the Grand Canyon line. Three Ambrose generations have served on this railroad. Will grew up in Williams while his father worked for the Santa Fe as a conductor and his son Roy worked as a brakeman with the railroad.

Brian Alexander had already scouted the availability of motive power and rolling stock but Max and Gary needed to travel and inspect them for purchase. This travel literally took them halfway around the world for China seemed to be the best bet for vintage locomotives in good running condition. Negotiations for the purchase of several American Baldwin locomotives had progressed reasonably well when student unrest and the massacre of Tiananmen Square caused a government upheaval which made further dealings impossible.

Other purchase or lease arrangements then became necessary and finally the company purchased four vintage 1906-10 Alco 2-8-0 Consolidation type locomotives in July. Numbers 18, 19 and 20 came from John Slack's Lake States Steam Transportation Company at Laona, Wisconsin. Steve Mattox of Council Bluffs, Iowa who owned No. 29 also agreed to sell. Originally built for the Lake Superior & Ishpemming Railroad, numbers 18, 19, 20 and 29 hauled iron ore from their date of delivery to 1960. Then sold to the Marquette and Huron Mountain Railroad number 19 worked the scenic line and the others remained in storage until 1985 when sold to Slack and Mattox. Company crews prepared all four for the move to Arizona and did some additional work on number 18 in Laona. Owing to delays caused by the Chicago and Northwestern, the engines and tenders did not arrive in Williams until late in August.

It seemed an impossible task to have number 18 ready for service on the 17th of September. But owing to a thorough knowledge of their craft and a willingness to work twenty hour days, the enginemen had her rolling at 1:23 AM on the 17th.

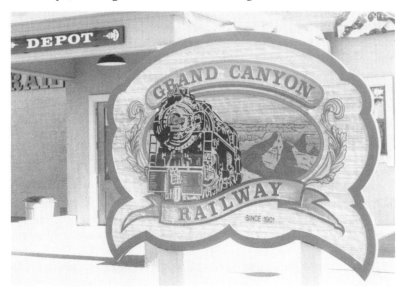

The Grand Canyon Railway logo welcomes passengers and visitors to the depot in Williams.

Completion of testing in the early morning hours had to be done in time to couple her to the passenger cars waiting in the station at 11:30 for a 12:00 noon departure. Volunteer assistance also played a part in making No. 18 ready for the big day. Staff, family and friends helped with the detail painting of the wheels, running boards, windows and polishing the brass bell and whistle which relieved the enginemen for the more skilled mechanical work. For everyone involved it was an incredible feat of stamina and workmanship!

Passenger cars for service on the line had been selected by Brian Alexander during his time with Railroad Resources. The seventeen 1923 vintage Pullman built Harriman style cars from the Southern Pacific yards in Oakland needed a complete overhaul and refit due to their advanced state of disrepair and decay. Car superintendent Bryan Reese selected seven in the best condition and made arrangement for their transport to the Tucson car shops of Pacific Fruit Express. The remainder went to Richmond, California for overhaul of their trucks and eventual shipment to Williams.

After the cars arrived in Tucson on 15 April Reese hired Greg Griffin as foreman and work crews to complete the necessary stripping and rebuilding of the rolling stock. As with the locomotive the cars had to be ready by the 17th of September. The crew removed all furnishings, windows, fixtures and electrical systems and then sand blasted years of paint and rust from the exterior. Metal repair and preparation for painting then followed. After exterior painting in the PFE shops the cars then needed a new electrical system, windows installed, wood refinished, interior painted and seats reupholstered and reinstalled. Their hard work paid off when the cars complete with "Grand Canyon" in gold letters arrived in Williams on 10 September.

From the beginning bricks and mortar became an integral part of the overall plan. This project involves considerably more than the rehabilitation of the railroad. Rehabilitation or new building construction moved forward concurrent with work on the locomotive and cars. The Fray Marcos Hotel and the depot had been allowed to deteriorate into a derelict structure. Considerable work needed to be done before it became ready to accept the role of the southern terminus of the line on the 17th of September. A new engine and car repair facility also began to take shape along with fuel and water storage tanks.

The Fray Marcos and depot presented a challenge to all involved. Tim Rogers, Director of Construction, established his crews around Bill Lockwood and Pete Otero. Carpenters, concrete workers, electricians, equipment operators, masons, plumbers and welders all became a daily part of the work. Cleaning up the mess left by years of vandalism turned out to be a major project in itself. The building is on the National Register of Historic Places and salvage and preservation of the remaining artifacts and significant components received every consideration. Almost all of the furnishings and fixtures had been sold off by the Santa Fe when the buildings had been retired but several documents and other significant items came to light. Exterior and interior walls required sandblasting to remove years of grime and paint. In this process the original layers of paint surfaced and restoration of the building color scheme to its 1908 finish began. The wooden windows had deteriorated to the extent salvage became impossible. Modern metal sashes constructed to look exactly like their wooden forebears replaced the old windows. Tons of cinders needed to be removed from the flat concrete roof before a peaked roof could be constructed to handle the winter snows and monsoon storms. Rehabilitation began on 29 March and continued right up to the time of opening on the 16th of September.

New construction of the engine and car facility began at the same time along the main line on the north side of town. This metal frame structure required many tons of concrete to be poured for the floors and drop pits used to service the power and rolling stock of the line. As the building took shape the laying of rails into and through it from the main line left no doubt as to the purpose of this structure. Contracted welders, using cranes and a spider web of scaffolds, assembled a 760,000 gallon steel water storage tank just to the north of the engine and car facility. After installation of a water-softening unit, the tank held effluent water piped over from the City of Williams water treatment plant to the west of the main line. For conservation of the area's most precious resource, the company's steam locomotives use reclaimed water from Williams and the Grand Canyon. The engine facility became operational in December but the water tank lasted only until early in 1992 when it collapsed due to faulty welding. Water is now treated and pumped directly into water cars and tenders.

Beyond reconstruction of the railroad and equipment, a major facet of the overall operation is the marketing and sales of the railroad's services. Concurrent with the rebuilding, others developed the sales program, reservations center, special promotions and media campaigns. Regularly generated news releases to the newspapers, TV and radio allowed the public to follow the progress of the railroad and learn of the services offered. On opening day of the reservations center the staff received over two hundred calls. By the middle of September the fall inaugural season from 18 September to 1 January approached being sold out. Additionally, group bookings of up to seven thousand passengers had been made for the 1990 season. The sales and special programs required entirely new graphics. Logos, brochures, tickets, flyers and signs using photos and artwork had to be designed and prepared for distribution. Gini Alexander focused on this work and produced all of these items usually with last minute notice and impossible deadlines.

Media interest increased daily with arrival of locomotives and coach cars. Articles in newspapers across the State of Arizona appeared daily. Major television news programs across the country carried news of the rebirth of the Grand Canyon Railway. When the 17th of September arrived marketing had attained its goal of domestic and international recognition of the project. Coverage of the re-inaugural event appeared in nearly every major daily newspaper and on most televison and radio networks. International magazines and newspapers from Switzerland to Japan also carried news of the grand reopening of the line. The Grand Canyon Railway certainly now held the position of an internationally recognized attraction.

The work required to get the train from Williams to the Grand Canyon came as a team effort. Everyone in the company had to pull together in order to attain the goal. Office personnel handled the daily administrative duties and thousands of tele-

This Santa Fe overpass near Prescott tells another story. The Grand Canyon line never went away completely.

phone calls. Food and beverage department personnel planned the food service and prepared train attendants for their duties. The accounting department kept track of expenditures, disbursed funds and paid salaries. Museum staff located artifacts and prepared displays. Maintenance crews cleaned up the Fray Marcos and put decorations in place. Gift shop items needed to be identified, purchased and displayed by the retail department. Programs had to be planned for all of the events and preparations made for the ceremonies. None of these things could be done by one individual or even one group of people. In the best can-do spirit, the Grand Canyon Railway people made the dream come true.

And, after ten years of hard work and an infusion of $28 million, many improvements are in evidence. Motive power rebuilding and additions have considerably increased the size, variety, and quality of the roster. The magnificent new 196-room Fray Marcos Hotel and Max & Thelma's Restaurant are reminiscent of Fred Harvey's first class service. Farwest Airlines, a companion company to GCRy, entered into service in 1999 and delivers passengers to Northern Arizona from a variety of Southwestern locations. The Grand Canyon Railway has come a long way from those first hectic days and more is yet to come.

Observers in 1989 witnessed frantic activity around the railroad in preparation for the running of the reinaugural. During a more liesurely time, in the 1950s, a mountain lion patiently waited for the train every morning around milepost thirty-five and sat beside the tracks looking for food thrown by the crew. She has long since disappeared but maybe her offspring will hear the whistle and resume the vigil. Today's passengers ride comfortably in 1923 Harriman style chair cars and 1950s vintage dome, parlor and chair cars. They listen attentively to the steam engines barkin' up a grade or the power of the Alco diesels. Many take pleasure in the mournful echos of the steam whistle while they travel through the trees and canyons or the raucus diesel air horns at a grade crossing. But, maybe all of those echos are not from the whistle. Some might be the welcoming cries of the ghost of the big cat who waited so many years for these trains to return.

Buckey O'Neill never rode the first train to the Canyon in 1901. If his spirit is as active as he had been in life it is almost a certainty that Buckey is a part of the new Grand Canyon Railway. Maybe he rides in the cab of every engine or walks the cars to greet the passengers on "his" railroad. What he did not get to enjoy in life he can now share with the newer generations of visitors to travel this line. Hang on Buckey! We're still on a roll!

GLOSSARY

This partial list of railroad terms and slang covers only those used in this text. Several good, complete glossaries are available for those interested in learning the language of the railroader.

Air brake: Brakes operated by air pressure.

Air man: A hoghead with better than average feel for the use of air brakes and the control of the train.

Block: Designated length of track between signals.

Boiler: Metal tank in which water is converted to steam by heat from the firebox.

Book of rules: Handbook of company rules and regulations.

Brakeman: Operates manual brakes on individual cars and throws switches.

Cab: Control compartment of a locomotive with engineer on the right and fireman on the left.

Clearance: Authorization for train movement.

Conductor: Person in charge of a train.

Cornfield meet: Head-on collision.

Coupler: Heavy, steel mechanism at both ends of cars and locomotives for connecting them together.

Dinkey skinner: Engineer for a logging railroad.

Dirt track: Roadbed without ballast.

Division: Part of a railroad under the control of a superintendent and the location of a crew change stop.

Dynamic brake: Locomotive brake system using a conversion of momentum into heat by electrical means which in turn retards the speed of the locomotive.

Engine: Another word used for locomotive. Actually the power component of a steam locomotive.

Extra: Train not listed on the printed schedule.

Gandy dancer: Track worker. Received this name from the use of Gandy Company track tools.

Grab irons: Hand railings on rolling stock used for a hand hold during mounting, dismounting or riding on the side.

Highball: Hand or oral signal to move a train and also used to indicate "moving fast."

Hog: A locomotive.

Hoghead: Locomotive engineer. The person trained to run a locomotive.

Hostler: Person who services locomotives.

In the ditch: Train that has been wrecked.

Join the birds: To jump from a moving engine or car usually just prior to a wreck.

Local: Freight train which sets out, picks up and switches cars in a given area or district.

Locomotive: Power unit of a train. For steam it consisted of an engine and a tender.

On the ground: Off the tracks. Derailed power or rolling stock.

Passing track: Siding to allow passing of trains on a single track main line.

Pilot: Wedge shaped metal barrier at the front of a steam locomotive and at both ends of a diesel to push aside obstacles on the track. A "cowcatcher."

Power: General term for locomotives.

Rail: Trainman. One of a pair of steel bars that make up a railroad track for the purpose of providing a running surface for the wheels of locomotives and cars.

Relay rail: Rail removed from one location and relaid at another location. Salvaged rail.

Road: Main line track.

Road bed: Bed upon which the ties, rails and ballast of the railroad track lies.

Roadmaster: Division officer responsible for keeping the track in his division in good repair.

Rolling stock: All wheeled equipment used on a railroad track.

Schedule: Printed timetable that gives number, class, direction and route for a train.

Section: One of two or more regular trains running on the same schedule. Also length of track to be maintained by a section gang.

Section gang: Crew of track workers usually used to maintain a specific length or section of track.

Shoofly: Temporary bypass track around damaged or obstructed track.

Siding: Track adjacent to the main line, usually with a switch at both ends, for the purpose of passing trains (passing track) or setting out rolling stock.

Single track: Main track on which trains are operated in both directions.

Spot: Position a piece of rolling stock for work, loading or unloading.

Spur: Track with only one switch.

Station: Place designated by name in the schedule.

Switch: Rail device with movable rails used to turn rolling stock from one track to another.

Tender: Storage component of a locomotive which carried fuel and water.

Torpedo: Explosive device placed upon the rail to warn an approaching train of danger ahead.

Tractive force: Energy transferred from locomotive's drivers to the rails.

Train: Coupled rolling stock operating under orders.

Truck: Wheel-axle assemblies upon which power and rolling stock rests and which causes it to be guided along the rails.

Turnout: Switch.

Unit: Complete diesel-electric locomotive or support section to a lead unit.

Varnish: Passenger train. From the days of varnished wooden cars.

Work extra: Train with materials and equipment for maintenance or construction.

BIBLIOGRAPHY

PERSONAL INTERVIEWS

ACOSTA, Jose A., Atchison, Topeka and Santa Fe Railway
    Section Foreman, Flagstaff, Arizona
ALEXANDER, Brian K., Former Vice President, Grand Canyon
    Railway, Flagstaff, Arizona
AMBROSE, Wilfred G., Baldwin Locomotive Works Design
    Engineer, Atchison, Topeka and Santa Fe Railway
    Locomotive Engineer, Phoenix, Arizona
BABBITT, John G., President, CO Bar Livestock Company,
    Flagstaff, Arizona
BIEGERT, Max L., Chairman and CEO, Grand Canyon Railway,
    Williams, Arizona
BIEGERT, Thelma, Secretary-Treasurer, Grand Canyon
    Railway, Williams, Arizona
BLACK, John L., Coconino County Deputy Sheriff, Longtime
    Resident of Williams and Flagstaff, Arizona
BLACK, Vera Goss, Teacher, Longtime Resident of Grand
    Canyon, Tusayan and Williams, Arizona
BLAIR, Cherrie L., Rancher, Lifelong Resident of Williams and
    Valle, Arizona
BLAIR, David F., Rancher, Lifelong Residents of Williams and
    Valle, Arizona
BRADLEY, John D., Head of Grand Canyon Mule College,
    Longtime Resident of Grand Canyon, Arizona
CARTLEDGE, Thomas R., United States Forest Service
    Archaeologist, Kaibab National Forest, Arizona
CHACON, Thomas R., United States Forest Service District
    Ranger, Kaibab National Forest, Arizona
CHAMBERS, W. David, President, Grand Canyon Railway,
    Flagstaff, Arizona
CHAPPELL, Gordon S., National Park Service Western
    Regional Historian, San Francisco, California
CHRISTMAN, Warren C., Atchison, Topeka and Santa Fe
    Railway Communications Technician, Williams, Arizona
COOK, Martha K., Grand Canyon Railway Passenger,
    Flagstaff, Arizona
CORONA, Gil, Atchison, Topeka and Santa Fe Railway Section
    Hand, Williams, Arizona
CRAVEY, Mary Lockridge, Lifelong Resident of Grand Canyon,
    Anita and Williams, Arizona
CURRY, George G., Atchison, Topeka and Santa Fe Railway
    Field Engineer, Williams, Arizona

DAVIS, John H., Superintendent, Grand Canyon National Park, Arizona

DUFFIELD, George A., Atchison, Topeka and Santa Fe Railway Maintenance, Escondido, California

FLOHRSCHUTZ, Gene, Atchison, Topeka and Santa Fe Railway Regional Manager Public Relations, Los Angeles, California

FULLER, Lester H., Cattleman, Sheepman, Lifelong Resident of Northern Arizona

GARLAND, Robert G., Atchison, Topeka and Santa Fe Railway Division Engineer, Phoenix, Arizona

GIPSON, Clifford G., Atchison, Topeka and Santa Fe Railway Bridge & Building Foreman, Phoenix, Arizona

GIPSON, Marie Burbank, Atchison, Topeka and Santa Fe Railway Telegrapher, Phoenix, Arizona

IRVIN, Glenn W., Atchison, Topeka and Santa Fe Railway Station Master, Williams, Arizona

KUHN, Millard E., Secretary-Treasurer, Arizona Lumber and Timber Company, Flagstaff, Arizona

LAUGER, William, United States Forest Service Landscape Architect, Kaibab National Forest, Arizona

LaCIVITA, Robert, Vice President, Operations, Grand Canyon Railway, Flagstaff, Arizona

MANN, Walter G., United States Forest Service Supervisor, Kaibab National Forest, Arizona

MATSON, Harry E., Lifelong Resident of Apex and Williams, Arizona

MACAULEY, Michael P., Northern Arizona Rancher, Coconino County Deputy Sheriff, Longtime Resident of Williams and Flagstaff, Arizona

MELICK, Dermont W., Dr., Longtime Resident of Williams, Arizona

MOORE, Grace Lockridge, Resident of Grand Canyon, Anita and Williams, Arizona

NICHOLAS, Daniel A., Fred Harvey Company Fire and Safety Supervisor, Grand Canyon, Arizona

NEWMAN, Charles R., President, Railroad Resources, Inc., Phoenix, Arizona

OSWALD, William E., Educator, Longtime resident of Williams, Arizona

PEARSON, Helen, Author, Lifelong Resident of Williams, Arizona

PERRIN, Lilo M., Northern Arizona Rancher, Lifelong Resident of Williams, Arizona

225

PLESE, Sonny J., Atchison, Topeka and Santa Fe Railway
Engineering Technician, Winslow, Arizona
POLSON, Kenneth M., Fred Harvey Company Bus Driver,
Lifelong Resident of Williams, Arizona
POUQUETTE, Marjorie H., School Teacher, Lifelong Resident
of Williams, Arizona
RIKER, David F., Burlington Northern Santa Fe Railway,
Director Administration, Arizona Division, Winslow,
Arizona
ROTH, Robert I., Former President, Grand Canyon Railway,
Williams, Arizona
SAMSON, Pauline J., School Teacher, Lifelong Resident of
Williams, Arizona
SANDOVAL, Juan, Atchison, Topeka and Santa Fe Railway
Section Foreman, Williams, Arizona
SCHMITZ, Eugene L., Atchison, Topeka and Santa Fe Railway
Locomotive Engineer, Winslow, Arizona
SETTERLAND, John, Saginaw and Manistee Lumber Company
Locomotive Engineer, Williams, Arizona
SMITH, Robert W., Atchison, Topeka and Santa Fe Railway
Hostler, Cowboy, Lifelong Resident of Williams, Arizona
SPIVEY, Mahlon E., Atchison, Topeka and Santa Fe Railway
Roadmaster, Phoenix, Arizona
SULLIVANT, R. Howard, Businessman, Lifelong Resident of
Williams, Arizona
SUTTON, William B., Atchison, Topeka and Santa Fe Railway
Locomotive Engineer, Justice of the Peace, Williams,
Arizona
THURSTON, Leland E. ("Bill"), Cattleman, Miner,
Businessman, Longtime Resident of Tusayan, Arizona
TURNER, Eloise Fain, Teacher, Author, Longtime Resident of
Grand Canyon and Clarkdale, Arizona
VERKAMP, Jack, Businessman, Lifelong Resident of Northern
Arizona, Grand Canyon, Arizona
WADSWORTH, Manley, Atchison, Topeka and Santa Fe
Railway Section Hand, New Oraibi, Arizona
WAMBLE, John T., Atchison, Topeka and Santa Fe Railway
Station Agent, Williams, Arizona
WAY, Thomas E. ("Spike"), Author, Justice of the Peace,
Longtime Resident of Williams, Arizona
WHITE, Ervin H., Trainmaster, Grand Canyon Railway,
Williams, Arizona
WILSON, Woodrow E., Saginaw and Manistee Lumber
Company Commissary Supervisor, Flagstaff, Arizona

CORRESPONDENCE

ARIZONA HERITAGE CENTER, Historical Repository,
Arizona Historical Society, Tucson, Arizona
ARIZONA BUREAU OF GEOLOGY AND MINERAL
TECHNOLOGY, Geological Survey Branch, Tucson,
Arizona
CHAMBERLIN, Edward M., National Park Service Museum
Technician, Grand Canyon, Arizona
GEHRT, Robert E., Atchison, Topeka and Santa Fe Railway
Assistant Vice President Public Relations, Chicago, Illinois
GLOVER, Vernon J., Southwestern Historian, Albuquerque,
New Mexico
MALLIN BROTHERS IRON AND METAL COMPANY, Scrap
Dealers, Phoenix, Arizona
MARTIN, Michael A., Atchison, Topeka and Santa Fe Railway
Manager of Public Affairs, Los Angeles, California
MENNINGER, Constance L., Santa Fe Archivist, Kansas State
Historical Society, Topeka, Kansas
MOORE, John B. Jr., Railroad Historian, Albuquerque, New
Mexico.
MYRICK, David F., Author, Railroad Historian, Santa Barbara,
California
REES, David I., Railroad Historian, Ajo, Arizona
SHINE, Joseph W., Author, Railroad Historian, La Mirada,
California
TORPIN, Q. W., Atchison, Topeka and Santa Fe Railway
General Manager, Los Angeles, California
WAHMANN, Russell, Author, Railroad Historian, Cottonwood,
Arizona

PUBLICATIONS AND DOCUMENTS

ARIZONA DEPARTMENT OF MINERAL RESOURCES,
Phoenix, Arizona.
ARIZONA STATE ARCHIVES, Phoenix, Arizona.
ATCHISON, TOPEKA AND SANTA FE RAILWAY, 1897-1921,
Contracts, correspondence and documents. Topeka: Office
of the Secretary- Treasurer.
ATCHISON, TOPEKA AND SANTA FE RAILWAY, 1908-
present, *Santa Fe Employees Magazine.* Los Angeles:
Public Relations Department.
ATCHISON, TOPEKA AND SANTA FE RAILWAY, *1902. Titan
of Chasms; The Grand Canyon of Arizona.* Chicago:
Passenger Department.

BALDWIN LOCOMOTIVE WORKS, 1906. *The Atchison, Topeka and Santa Fe Railway System; Record of Recent Construction #56.* Philadelphia.

BRADLEY, Glenn D., 1920. *The Story of the Santa Fe to 1920s.* Boston: The Gorham Press.

BURPEE, C. Miles, 1945. *Railway Engineering & Maintenance Cyclopedia.* Chicago: Simmons-Boardman Publishing Corp.

CALIFORNIA STATE RAILROAD MUSEUM LIBRARY, Sacramento, California.

COCONINO SUN, THE, Newspaper of Flagstaff, Arizona.

CHAPPELL, Gordon S., 1976. "Railroad at the Rim; The Origin and Growth of the Grand Canyon Village." *Journal of Arizona History,* 17:89-107.

CLINE, Platt, 1976. *They Came to the Mountain.* Flagstaff: Northern Arizona University.

COCONINO COUNTY ASSESSOR. Flagstaff, Arizona.

COCONINO COUNTY RECORDER. Flagstaff, Arizona.

DARTON, N. H. and others, 1916. *Guidebook of the Western United States, Part C, The Santa Fe Route.* Department of the Interior and the United States Geological Survey Bulletin 613.

FUCHS, James R., 1953. *A History of Williams, Arizona 1876-1951.* University of Arizona Bulletin, #23. Tucson.

GAMST, Frederick C., 1980. *The Hoghead.* Boston: Holt, Rinehart and Winston.

GENERAL SOIL MAP, Coconino County, Arizona, 1972. United States Department of Agriculture, Soil Conservation Service.

GORNITZ, V. and KERR, P. F., 1970. "Uranium Mineralization and Alteration." *Economic Geology,* 65:751-68.

GRATTAN, Virginia L., 1980. *Mary Colter; Builder Upon the Red Earth.* Flagstaff: Northland Press.

HAY, Oliver P., 1922. "Descriptions of Species of Pleistocene Vertebrata; 5. Collection of Fossil Mammals Made At Anita, Coconino County, Arizona." *Proceedings of the U. S. National Museum,* 59:617-638.

HIGGINS, G. A., 1901. *Grand Canyon.* Chicago: Atchison, Topeka and Santa Fe Railway Company.

HUGHES, J. Donald, 1967. *The Story of Man at the Grand Canyon.* Grand Canyon Natural History Association.

HUGHES, J. Donald, 1978. *In the House of Stone and Light.* Grand Canyon Natural History Association.

JAMES, George Wharton, 1900. *In and Around the Grand Canyon.* Boston: Little, Brown and Company.

KANSAS STATE HISTORICAL SOCIETY, Topeka, Kansas.

KOCH, Michael, 1971. *The Shay Locomotive; Titan of the Timber.* Denver: World Press, Inc.

LINDSAY, E. H. and TESSMAN, N. R., 1974. Cenozoic Vertebrate Localities and Faunas in Arizona. *Journal of the Arizona Academy of Science,* 9:3-24.

MUIR, John, 1902. "The Grand Canyon of the Colorado." *Century Illustrated Monthly Magazine,* November:107-16.

NATIONS, J. D. and STUMP, Edmund, 1981. *Geology of Arizona.* Dubuque: Kendall/Hunt.

NATIONS, J. D., LANDYE, J. J. and HEVLY, R. H., 1982. "Location and Chronology of Tertiary Sedimentary Deposits in Arizona: A Review." *In* Ingersoll, R. V. and Woodburn, M. O. (eds.), Cenozoic Nonmarine Deposits of California and Arizona: Pacific Section. S.E.P.M. 107-122.

MUSEUM OF NORTHERN ARIZONA, Flagstaff, Arizona.

NORTHERN ARIZONA UNIVERSITY, Cline Library Special Collections and Archives. Flagstaff, Arizona.

RICHMOND, Albert J. Jr., 1987. *Historic Precipitation Sequences on the Colorado Plateau, 1859-1983* . MS Thesis, Northern Arizona University.

SCARBOROUGH, Robert B., 1980. "Breccia Pipe Sources." *Fieldnotes,* Vol 10, 4:3-4.

SCARBOROUGH, Robert B., 1981. "Radioactive Occurances and Uranium Production in Arizona." Report prepared for USDE by the Arizona Bureau of Geology, 43-50.

SHARLOT HALL MUSEUM, Prescott, Arizona

SMITH, Jack, 1984. *Tales of the Beale Road.* Flagstaff: Tales of the Beale Road Publishing Company.

SULLIVANT, R. Howard. Copies of the *Williams News,* 1886-1901.

SURAN, Charles W., 1989. *With the Wings of an Angel.* Flagstaff: unpublished manuscript.

UNITED STATES DEPARTMENT of the INTERIOR, Bureau of Land Management. Phoenix, Arizona. Government Land Office Maps and Surveyors Field Notes.

UNITED STATES GEOLOGICAL SURVEY. Flagstaff, Arizona. Maps and Surveys.

WAESCHE, Hugh, 1933. "The Anita Copper Mine." *Grand CanyonNature Notes,* 7:108-112.

WAY, Thomas E., 1980. *Summary of Travel to the Grand Canyon.* Prescott: Prescott Graphics.

WILLIAMS NEWS, Newspaper of Williams, Arizona. Copies of papers from 1901 to present.

WISBEY, Herbert A., 1946. *The History of the Santa Fe Railroad in Arizona to 1917*. Tucson: MA Thesis, University of Arizona.

WORLEY, E. Dale, 1965. *Iron Horses of the Santa Fe Trail*. Dallas: Southwest Railroad Historical Society.

PHOTOGRAPHS

AMBROSE, Wilfred G.
ANDERLE, Deanna L.
ATCHISON, TOPEKA AND SANTA FE RAILWAY COMPANY
AVERY, Valeen Tippetts
BASSETT, Gordon Cole
BLACK, John L.
CHAPPELL, Gordon S.
COLEMAN, John D.
COOK, Martha K.
CRAVEY, Mary Lockridge
CURRY, George G.
DUFFIELD, George A.
JAMES, Rosemary C.
LUCKESEN, John J.
MACAULEY, Michael P.
MATSON, Harry E.
McCARTER, Malcolm D.
MELICK, Dermont W., Dr.
MOORE, Grace Lockridge
MUSEUM OF NORTHERN ARIZONA
NORTHERN ARIZONA UNIVERSITY, Cline Library Special Collections and Archives
OSWALD, William
PEARSON, Helen
POLSON, Kenneth M.
SAMSON, Pauline J.
SAN BERNARDINO RAILROAD HISTORICAL SOCIETY
SCHMITZ, Eugene L.
SEAMAN, Jacquelyn A.
SULLIVANT, R. Howard
TURNER, Eloise Fain
UNITED STATES DEPARTMENT of AGRICULTURE, Forest Service
UNITED STATES DEPARTMENT of the INTERIOR, National Park Service
WILLIAMS NEWS